Streamline ENGLISH

BERNARD HARTLEY & PETER VINEY

CONNECTIONS

An intensive English course for
pre-intermediate students

Oxford University Press

Oxford University Press
Walton Street, Oxford OX2 6DP

Oxford London Glasgow New York Toronto
Melbourne Wellington Cape Town Nairobi
Dar Es Salaam Kuala Lumpur Singapore Hong Kong
Tokyo Delhi Bombay Calcutta Madras Karachi

ISBN 0 19 432227 0 (student's edition)
ISBN 0 19 432228 9 (teacher's edition)
ISBN 0 19 432229 7 (set of two cassettes)
© Oxford University Press 1979
First published 1979
Sixth impression 1982

Illustrations by:

Alan Austin   Paddy Mounter
Stephen Crisp   Terry Pastor
Julian Graddon   Gary Rees
Alun Hood   Elly Robinson
Alan Lawrence   Bill Sanderson
Edward McLachlan   Brian Sweet
Brian Moore   Ken Thompson
Richard Morris

Photographs by:
Vernon Brooke   Terry Williams
Billett Potter

The publishers would like to thank the following for
their time and assistance:
R. R. Alden & Son Ltd   House of Tweed, Oxford
Barclays Bank Ltd   Luna Caprese Restaurant
Bollom Ltd   New Theatre, Oxford
Boots The Chemists   Oxford Illustrators Ltd
Glyn Brown   H. Samuel Ltd
Charmers Hair Craft   J. Summersell
City of Oxford Motor   Sunshine Records
  Services Ltd   Thames Valley Police
Debenhams

The publishers would like to thank the following for
permission to reproduce photographs:
All-Sport Photographic Ltd
Pat Brindley
British Airways
Photographic Department, B L Cars, Cowley
British Petroleum Co Ltd
Lance Brown
Colour Library International Ltd
Colorific Photo Library
Colorsport
Gerry Cranham
Mary Evans Picture Library
Alan Hutchison Library
Keystone Press Agency Ltd
London Features International Ltd
The Mansell Collection
Paul Popper Ltd
Rolls Royce Motors Ltd
Syndication International Ltd
The Times Newspapers Ltd

Set in Palatino and Helvetica by
Filmtype Services Limited, Scarborough

Printed in Hong Kong by
Hip Shing Offset Printing Factory

The authors would like to thank all the people who helped in the development of this book. In particular we are grateful to the Directors of the Anglo-Continental Educational Group, and Chris Goodchild, Director of Studies, Anglo-Continental School of English, Bournemouth, for all their support and encouragement. We also wish to thank all our colleagues in the ACEG schools who provided invaluable comments and criticism. Particular thanks are due to Stephanie Miles who illustrated the pilot edition.

Students can buy a cassette which
contains a recording of the texts
and dialogues in this book.

1 All Aboard!

The *Southampton* is cruising around the Mediterranean Sea. There are a lot of tourists on the ship. Most of them are English, but some of them are American, Australian, or Canadian. It's the sixth day of the cruise, and their ship is sailing from Genoa to Naples. All of the passengers and most of the crew are on deck for the Captain's party.

A Hello. My name's Charles Beatty.
  I'm from Chicago.
B Pleased to meet you.
  I'm Wendy Hillman.
A Where do you come from?
B I come from Stirling.
A Oh, where's that?
B It's in Scotland.

Questions

What is the *Southampton* doing?
Are all of the passengers English?
Ask "How many of them . . .?"
Where are the others from?
Is it the first day of the cruise?
Ask "Which day?"
Where's the ship?
Where are the passengers?
Why are they there?

C What an awful party!
D Oh, do you think so?
C Yes, I do. Oh, by the way, my name's
   Green.
D My name's Nelson . . . .
C I work in a bank. What do you do?
D Well, I'm the captain of this ship. It's
   my party.
C Oh, I'm terribly sorry!

E Would you like another drink?
F Pardon?
E Would you like another drink?
F Oh, yes, please . . . I'd like an orange
   juice.
E With ice?
F No, thanks.

Exercise 1

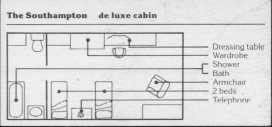

The Southampton   Boarding Card

Surname	Forename(s)
Nationality	Date of birth
Profession	Permanent address
Signature	Date

All of the passengers had to complete this card.
Here are some of the questions:
What's your surname?
What are your forenames?
When were you born?
What nationality are you?
What do you do?
Where do you live?
Ask somebody these questions, and complete
the card for them.

Exercise 2

This is a 'de luxe' cabin on the *Southampton*.
There are two beds, and there's a shower . . . .
Describe the cabin.

The Southampton   de luxe cabin

Dressing table
Wardrobe
Shower
Bath
Armchair
2 beds
Telephone

Exercise 3

The Southampton   Itinerary

GENOA
CANNES
BARCELONA
NAPLES
CORFU
GIBRALTAR
PALMA
ATHENS
MALTA
RHODES
ALEXANDRIA

Itinerary
Saturday 1st	Gibraltar
Sunday 2nd	Palma
Monday 3rd	Barcelona
Tuesday 4th	Cannes
Wednesday 5th	Genoa
Thursday 6th	Naples
Friday 7th	Malta
Saturday 8th	Corfu
Sunday 9th	Athens
Monday 10th	Rhodes
Tuesday 11th	Alexandria

Where have they been?
When did they go there?
Where haven't they been yet?
Where are they going?
When are they going there?

2 Telephoning

A Directory Enquiries. Which town, please?
B Oxford.
A What name, please?
B Oxford University Press. Walton Street.
A That's Oxford 56767.
B Thank you. Can you tell me the code for Oxford?
A 0865.
B Thanks. Goodbye.

Directory Enquiries:
192

Reed, Clive,
7 High Street, Bath
12345 (0273)

MacDonald & Co.,
84 North Gate, York
23456 (0904)

Western Bank,
60 Ireland Road,
Liverpool
567 8901 (051)

C MacDonald and Company. . . . Can I help you?
D I'd like to speak to Mr Walker, please.
C Mr Walker? Which department is he in?
D Accounts.
C Hold on . . . trying to connect you . . . all right . . . you're through.

Mr Walker
 Accounts department
Miss Robbins
 Sales department
Mrs Cole
 Publicity department
Peter Brown
 Marketing department

F Number, please?
G Oh, I'd like to make a transferred charge call.
F Where to?
G Stratford.
F What number?
G 17414.
F What's your name, please?
G Joan Fitzgerald.
F Can you spell that?
G F-i-t-z-g-e-r-a-l-d.
F . . . and where are you calling from?
G 01-992-6636.
F Right. Hold the line, please.

Joan Fitzgerald
Bill McQueen
Sam Jenkins
Anita Bendix
Karen Waverly
Philip Hope

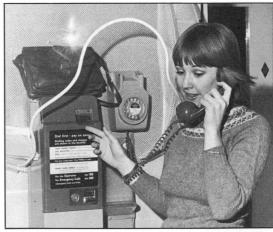

H Who are you telephoning?
I Nobody.
H Well, why are you holding the phone?
I My watch has stopped.
H I don't understand!
I I'm phoning the 'speaking clock' . . . listen . . . (At the third stroke, it will be 8.52 and 30 seconds.)

Speaking clock 8081

Weather (London Area) 01-246-8091

Tourist information (London) 01-246-8041

Business News 01-246-8026

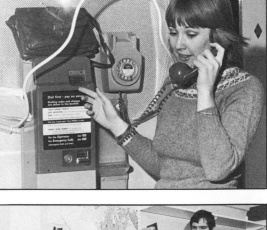

3 Fizz is fantastic!

Ian Peters: Let's meet Mrs Edna Campbell, from Glasgow. This is her kitchen, and on the table there are two piles of dirty clothes. Mrs Campbell's got three young children and she has to do a lot of washing. Now, we've got two identical 'British Electric' automatic washing machines in the kitchen. Mrs Campbell's going to wash this pile of clothes in new 'Fizz' detergent, and that pile in another well-known washing powder.

Now both machines are working, and Mrs Campbell's making us a cup of tea!

Ian Ah, both machines have stopped, and she's taken the clothes out of them. Well, Mrs Campbell! What do you think?

Mrs C Well, I've washed these clothes in 'Fizz' and those clothes in the other powder.

Ian Can you see any difference?

Mrs C Ah, yes! These clothes are much cleaner. And they're whiter and softer than the others.

Ian These clothes? You washed these clothes in new 'Fizz'!

Mrs C That's right . . . oh, it's much better than my usual powder. My clothes have never been cleaner than this!

Ian Well . . . which powder are you going to buy next time?

Mrs C New 'Fizz', of course. It's the best powder I've ever used!

is best at the launderette too!

A lot of people haven't got washing machines. They take their clothes to the launderette.

Instructions:

1 Open the door, and load the machine with clothes.
2 Close the door securely, and put 'Fizz' into the soap compartment.
3 Select the washing temperature (hot or warm).
4 Put a 50p piece into the slot on the right.
5 The clothes are ready in 30 minutes.

Exercise

When you're waiting at the launderette, you can have a cup of coffee. Write instructions for the coffee machine.

HOT DRINKS

■ TEA

■ COFFEE

■ CHOCOLATE

■ MILK

■ SUGAR

Insert 5p
Insert cup
Wait 10 seconds

Reject coin

4 Olympic Report

Good evening. It's 11.15 . . . and it's time for 'Olympic Report'. Our report tonight is coming live by satellite from the Olympic Games.

Swimming

Good evening. Well, today's most important event was certainly the women's 200 metres freestyle. The American, Doris Kennedy, was first and got the gold medal. She swam the 200 metres in a new world record time of 1 minute 58 seconds. The U.S.A. won two gold medals yesterday, and three the day before, so in the first three days they've won six 'golds'.

Javelin

This is Jack Lumber from Canada. This morning he won the men's javelin final. At his first attempt he threw the javelin over 100 metres. Nobody has ever done this before. Unfortunately there was nearly a terrible accident in the javelin event. Henry Fraser, the British competitor, slipped when he was throwing his javelin and it hit a judge in the foot. Luckily, it didn't hurt him.

Gymnastics

Here we are in the Olympic Gymnasium. Olga Ivanov, the fifteen year old Russian gymnast, has just finished her display. We're waiting for the results now.

And here's the result! She's got an average of 9.5 points. That's the best score today! Olga's won the gold medal!

Exercise 1

The 21st Olympic Games were in Montreal in July, 1976.
Here are some of the records.
Men's Javelin – Nemeth (Hungary) 94.58 metres
Nemeth, the Hungarian, won the men's javelin competition. He threw it 94.58 metres.
Men's 800 metres – Juantorena (Cuba) 1 minute 43.5 seconds
Juantorena, the Cuban, won the men's 800 metres. He ran 800 metres in 1 minute 43.5 seconds.

Write sentences for:
Men's Long Jump – Beamon (U.S.A.) 8.9 metres
Men's Discus – Wilkins (U.S.A.) 68.28 metres
Women's 100 metres – Richter (West Germany) 11.01 seconds
Women's High Jump – Ackermann (East Germany) 1.93 metres
Men's Swimming (200 metres breaststroke) – Wilkie (Britain) 2 minutes 15.11 seconds
Men's Weightlifting (heavyweight) – Alexeev (U.S.S.R.) 440 kilos

High jump

We're just waiting for the last jumper. Ted Kelly, from Britain, is going to jump. The bar is at 2.30 metres.

Now he's beginning his final attempt . . .

And he's jumped.

Ooh! He's crashed into the bar!

He's landing. The bar's fallen. Is he hurt?

No, no, he's all right. He's getting up and walking away. But he's a very disappointed man.

Exercise 2

A *He's going to* lift *it*.   **B** *He's lifting it*.   **C** *He's lifted it*.
Write sentences:

A . . . jump.   **B** . . .   **C** . . .

A . . . throw . . .   **B** . . .   **C** . . .

5 I'll be there

A Psst! He'll be here tomorrow night . . .
B Will he? What time?
A About eight o'clock.
B Will he be at the station?
A No, he'll be at the airport.
B Right! I'll be there. Will he be alone?
A No, he won't. He'll be with his wife.
B Will you be there?
A Yes. I'll be outside in the white Rover.
B What about the money?
A Don't worry. It'll be there.
B O.K. I'll see you tomorrow night.

Exercise

A He'll be here tomorrow.
B *He won't be here tomorrow.*
C *Will he be here tomorrow?*

A They'll be there next week.
B . . .
C . . .

A . . .
B She won't be here next Monday.
C . . .

A . . .
B . . .
C Will you be here next year?

6 Monday morning

David What's the matter?

Sue Oh, I don't know.

David Oh, come on . . . it's something. What is it?

Sue It's just life . . . it's so boring.

David Oh, it's not so bad . . . you've got Daniel!

Sue But he's only a baby! It's all right for you. You'll leave the house in five minutes. I'll be here all day. When'll you come home? You won't come home till seven!

David One of us must go to work, dear.

Sue Yes, but your day'll be interesting. My day'll be the same as every day.

David My work isn't always interesting.

Sue I know, but you travel around, you meet different people and you do different things. Who'll I meet today? What'll I do? Eh? I'll wash up, feed the baby, do the washing, clean the house, bath the baby, take the dog for a walk. . . .

David But . . . but . . . dear.

Sue Then I'll go to the supermarket, prepare dinner, meet you at the station, have dinner, wash up again . . .

David But . . . but. . . dear.

Sue Then I'll feed the baby again, put the baby to bed . . . What a life! Today, tomorrow, this week, next week, this month, next month, next year . . . for ever!

David It's just Monday, dear . . . you'll be O.K. later.

Sue Will I?

His Monday
David Shaw, television interviewer

 8.30 catch the train
 9.30 arrive at the television studio
10.00 interview Miss World
12.00 have lunch with a film producer
 3.00 meet Paul McCartney at London Airport
 4.00 have cocktails at new discotheque
 5.00 catch the train
 7.30 have dinner
 8.30 watch television
 9.00 go to the pub

Her Monday
Sue Shaw, housewife

 9.00 wash up
10.00 feed the baby
10.30 do the washing
12.00 clean the house
 1.00 take the dog for a walk
 2.30 go to the supermarket
 4.00 prepare dinner
 5.30 meet David at the station
 7.30 have dinner
10.00 go to bed

Exercise 1

What'll he do at 8.30?
He'll catch the train.
Write questions and answers about David.

Exercise 2

When will she wash up?
She'll wash up at nine o'clock.
Write questions and answers about Sue.

7 Doctor Sowanso

Doctor Sowanso is the Secretary General of the United Nations. He's one of the busiest men in the world. He's just arrived at New Delhi Airport now. The Indian Prime Minister is meeting him. Later they'll talk about Asian problems.

Yesterday he was in Moscow. He visited the Kremlin and had lunch with Soviet leaders. During lunch they discussed international politics.

Tomorrow he'll fly to Nairobi. He'll meet the President of Kenya and other African leaders. He'll be there for twelve hours.

The day after tomorrow he'll be in London. He'll meet the British Prime Minister and they'll talk about European economic problems.

Next week he'll be back at the United Nations in New York. Next Monday he'll speak to the General Assembly about his world tour. Then he'll need a short holiday.

Questions

Who is Doctor Sowanso?
Where's he just arrived?
Who's meeting him?
What'll they talk about?

Where was he yesterday?
Who did he have lunch with?
What did they discuss?
When did he leave Moscow?

Where will he fly tomorrow?
Who will he meet?
How long will he be there?

When will he be in London?
Who will he meet?
What will they talk about?

Where will he be next week?
What will he do on Monday?
Why will he need a holiday?

8 Sleep and Dreams

Most people need eight hours' sleep.

1 How many hours do you need?
2 How many hours did you sleep last night?
3 Did you sleep well or badly?
4 Are you tired?
5 What time do you usually go to bed?
6 How about last night?
7 What time do you usually get up?
8 How about this morning?

Some people use
a) sleeping tablets
b) hot-water bottles
c) electric blankets

1 Do you use   a b c?
2 Have you ever used   a b c?
3 Why did you use   a b c?
4 Last night, did you use   a b c?

Some people sleep on their
a) backs
b) sides
c) fronts

1 How do you sleep?
2 Do you change position?

SLEEP AND DREAMS

Some people can sleep
a) on a train
b) on a plane
c) on a bus
d) in a chair
e) standing up

1 Can you? Have you ever?
2 When? Where?

Some people
a) snore in their sleep
b) walk in their sleep
c) talk in their sleep

1 Do you | snore in your sleep?
           | walk in your sleep?
           | talk in your sleep?
2 Have you ever snored/walked/talked in your sleep?
3 How do you know?

Everybody dreams every night.

1 Do you dream in black and white, or colour?
2 Do you always/sometimes/rarely remember your dreams?
3 Have you ever had a nightmare?/a running dream?/a falling dream?/a flying dream?

9 At the chemist's

A Good afternoon.
B Good afternoon. Can I help you?
A Yes. I've got a terrible headache.
B How long have you had it?
A Only about two or three hours.
B Well, try these tablets. Take two with water every three hours.
A Thank you very much.

headache
stomach-ache
back-ache
ear-ache
sore throat
cold

tablets
capsules
pills

C Good morning.
D Good morning. I'd like a toothbrush please.
C Nylon or natural bristle?
D Nylon, please.
C Hard, soft, or medium?
D Medium, please.
C What colour would you like?
D It doesn't matter really. . . . Oh, white's O.K.
C There you are.

white
blue
red
green
yellow
pink

E Could I have a tube of toothpaste, please?
F With fluoride or without fluoride?
E With fluoride, please.
F Is that all, sir?
E Yes, that's all, thank you.
F Shall I put it in a bag?
E Please.

a tube of toothpaste
 with/without fluoride
a bar of soap
 large/small
a packet of razor
 blades five/ten
a jar of hand cream
 large/small
a box of tissues
 pocket size/man size
a roll of film
 35 mm/126/110
a tin of throat lozenges
 large/small

G Good evening.
H Good evening. Can you make up this prescription, please?
G Certainly. Would you like to wait?
H How long will it take?
G It'll be ready in twenty minutes.
H Oh, I'll come back later.
G All right, sir.
H Shall I pay now or later?
G Later'll be all right.

twenty minutes
a few minutes
a moment
an hour
half an hour

10 Lord Worth

Lord Worth Come in!
Mary Yes, sir?
Lord Worth No, no Mary . . . I don't want you!
Mary Who do you want, sir?
Lord Worth I want James . . . I want him immediately!
Mary Yes, sir . . . I'll go and find him.

Later

Lord Worth Ah, James!
James Did you want to see me, sir?
Lord Worth Yes, I wanted to see you twenty minutes ago.
James Sorry, sir. I was in the garage.
Lord Worth I want a car this afternoon.
James Which car do you want, sir? The Rolls, the Mercedes, or the Ferrari?
Lord Worth Mmm . . . the Rolls, I think . . . Yes, the Rolls.
James Where do you want to go, sir?
Lord Worth Heathrow Airport. Terminal 2.
James What time, sir?
Lord Worth We'll leave here after lunch . . . at two o'clock.

Later

Lord Worth Ah, Charles!
Charles Yes, sir.
Lord Worth I want an early lunch today, Charles.
Charles Yes, sir . . . What time?
Lord Worth Twelve o'clock . . . Oh, and I want you to reserve a table at the Savoy . . . for seven o'clock.
Charles Yes, sir.
Lord Worth . . . and I want Mary to prepare the guest room for Sir Thomas. I want her to make a special effort. Sir Thomas is a very important guest.
Charles Yes, sir . . . anything else, sir?
Lord Worth No, Charles, that's all.

Exercise 1

I wanted to do something.
What did you want to do?

1 They wanted to go somewhere.
2 He wanted to buy something.
3 We wanted to meet someone.
4 She wanted to eat something.
5 I wanted to see someone.

Exercise 2

He/her/cook the dinner.
He *wants* her *to* cook the dinner.

1 She/me/reserve a table.
2 I/him/help me.
3 They/her/clean the room.
4 My parents/me/learn English.
5 The police/them/stop.
6 She/me/dance.
7 The teacher/us/do our homework.

Exercise 3

When I was young, my father wanted me to be a doctor. He wanted me to work hard.

What did your | father | want you to do?
| mother |
| teachers |
What did you want to do?

11 Look, feel, taste, sound, smell

A I like your fur coat, Helen.
B Do you?
A Yes, it looks very expensive.
B Really? It wasn't expensive . . . it was second-hand.
A Was it? It doesn't look second-hand, it looks brand-new.

C Brrr! It feels cold in here.
D Does it?
C Yes . . . is the radiator on?
D Yes, it is. It'll feel warmer in a minute.

E Waiter! These vegetables aren't fresh!
F But they are fresh, sir.
E Well, they don't taste fresh to me.
F I'm sorry, sir . . . but . . .
E And the wine . . . it tastes sweet, and I asked for dry!
F I'll get the manager, sir.

H Listen to my new hi-fi, John. Does it sound all right?
G Yes, it sounds fine to me.
H I think the bass is too loud.
G No, it sounds perfect . . . it sounds better than mine.

I Have you changed your perfume?
J Yes, why? Do you like it?
I Yes, it smells terrific. What kind is it?
J It's 'Charlie'.
I It smells expensive. Is it?
J I don't know. It was a present.

12 A science fiction story

The spaceship flew around the new planet several times. The planet was blue and green. They couldn't see the surface of the planet because there were too many white clouds. The spaceship descended slowly through the clouds and landed in the middle of a green forest. The two astronauts put on their space suits, opened the door, climbed carefully down the ladder, and stepped onto the planet.

The woman looked at a small control unit on her arm. 'It's all right,' she said to the man. 'We can breathe the air . . . it's a mixture of oxygen and nitrogen.' Both of them took off their helmets and breathed deeply.

They looked at everything carefully. All the plants and animals looked new and strange. They couldn't find any intelligent life.

After several hours, they returned to their spaceship. Everything looked normal. The man switched on the controls, but nothing happened. 'Something's wrong,' he said. 'I don't understand . . . the engines aren't working.' He switched on the computer, but that didn't work either. 'Eve,' he said, 'we're stuck here . . . we can't take off!'

'Don't worry, Adam,' she replied. 'They'll rescue us soon.'

13 It's much too hot!

In the station buffet

Michael Come on, Susan! Hurry up! Drink your coffee! The train's leaving in a minute. We'll be late!

Susan I can't finish it. It's much too hot for me to drink.

Michael Why don't you put some milk in?

Susan I don't like white coffee . . . oh . . . O.K.

Michael There! Is it cool enough for you to drink now?

Susan Yes . . . but it tastes awful!

On the platform

Susan Oh! There's the train . . . bring the cases.

Michael Ooh! What have you got in these cases?

Susan Only clothes. Why? Are they heavy?

Michael Yes, they are!

Susan The taxi driver managed to carry them.

Michael Well, they're too heavy for me to carry.

Susan Well, I'm not strong enough to help you. . . . Porter!

On the train

Susan Oh, Michael . . . I didn't tell you. My sister phoned yesterday.

Michael Oh? Which sister? Andrea?

Susan Yes . . . she wants to get married.

Michael Married! But she isn't old enough to get married. She's only seventeen. Who's she going to marry?

Susan Basil Caraway.

Michael Basil Caraway! I don't believe it! He's much too old for her. He's over sixty!

Susan I know . . . but she loves him!

At their destination

Susan Oh, no! That was the last bus home! And we've missed it!

Michael Well, let's walk . . . it's a nice, warm evening.

Susan It's four miles! It's too far for me to walk. Call a taxi!

Michael A taxi! My name isn't Rockefeller! We aren't rich enough to travel everywhere by taxi.

Susan Michael! You've forgotten something!

Michael What?

Susan We've got three suitcases. Do you really want to walk?

Michael O.K. . . . O.K. . . . Taxi!

In the station buffet

On the platform

On the train

At their destination

Exercise 1

He can't lift it. It's very heavy.
It's too heavy for him to lift.

1 They can't drink it. It's very hot.
2 She can't buy it. It's too expensive.
3 He can't answer it. It's very difficult.
4 We can't see it. It's very small.

Exercise 2

Can he lift the boxes?
No, he isn't strong enough to lift them.

1 Can you touch the ceiling?	(tall)
2 Can they buy that house?	(rich)
3 Can he understand the questions?	(clever)
4 Can that cat catch the bird?	(quick)

14 A phone call

Mary Hello.
Mike Mary? Is that you?
Mary Yes. Mary here . . . Who's speaking?
Mike It's Mike.
Mary Mike? . . . Mike who?
Mike What do you mean 'Mike who?' . . . Mike Conners, of course.
Mary Oh, Mike . . . I'm sorry.
Mike Yes. We had a date last night. Where were you?
Mary Oh, I'm sorry, Mike. I couldn't come.
Mike Couldn't come! Why couldn't you come?
Mary Well, I had to wash my hair.
Mike Wash your hair! Why didn't you phone me?
Mary I wanted to phone you, but I couldn't remember your number.
Mike But it's in the telephone directory.
Mary Yes, I know, but I couldn't remember your surname.
Mike Oh . . . But why did you have to wash your hair last night?
Mary Well I had to do it last night because I'm going to the opera tonight.
Mike The opera! Who with?
Mary George . . . George Johnson . . . my boss's son.
Mike I see.
Mary He asked me yesterday. I didn't want to go but I couldn't say no.

Questions

Who's telephoning?
Who's answering the phone?
Did they have a date?
Ask "When?"
Why couldn't she come?
Did she want to phone him?
Why didn't she phone him?
Is his number in the directory?
Why couldn't she find it?
Did she have to wash her hair?
Ask "Why?"
Is she going to the opera with Mike?
Ask "Who . . . with?"
Did she want to go?
Why did she say yes?

15 Army Careers Office

Sergeant Good morning. Are you the new cleaner?

Briggs No. I'm not. I want to join the army.

Sgt. What! You! In the army?

Briggs Yes. I want to be a soldier. This is the Army Careers Office, isn't it?

Sgt. Well . . . er . . . yes. Sit down . . . sir.

Briggs Thanks.

Sgt. Now why do you want to be a soldier? Mr . . . Mr . . .

Briggs Briggs . . . Tommy Briggs. Well, I saw the 'ad' on television last night and it looked nice . . . holidays . . . money . . . girls . . . pension . . . travel.

Sgt. I see. Yes, it's a good life in the army . . . it's a man's life.

Briggs Ah!

Sgt. Now, have you got any questions?

Briggs Yes . . . will I have to get a haircut?

Sgt. A haircut. Oh yes, you'll have to get a haircut . . . and wear a uniform.

Briggs A uniform!

Sgt. Oh yes. And you'll have to obey orders. But you won't have to clean the toilets, you know. I've never had to clean the toilets.

Briggs What about the work? Will I have to work hard?

Sgt. Oh yes. You'll have to work hard . . . but all the girls like a man in uniform, you know.

Briggs And what about promotion?

Sgt. Oh yes. There are a lot of opportunities. Perhaps you'll be a general one day.

Briggs O.K. I'd like to join.

Sgt. Yes, sir. Just sign your name here.

Briggs There you are . . . Tommy Briggs.

Sgt. Briggs!

Briggs Eh?

Sgt. Shut up. Stand up. Straight. Now, quick march. Left . . . right . . . left . . . right . . . .

Exercise

A friend is going to join the army in your country. What will he have to do? What won't he have to do?

Write six sentences.

16 A traffic survey

The city of Oxford has got a traffic problem. It's an old town and the streets are narrow. There are too many cars and not enough parking spaces in the city centre. The Planning Department wanted to change the traffic system, and so they conducted a traffic survey. They asked a lot of people these five questions:

1 How old are you?
2 Can you drive?
3 How long have you been able to drive?
4 Where do you live?
5 How do you come to town?

Here are some of the results:

Mr Brown's fifty-eight.
He learned to drive when he was eighteen.
He's been able to drive for forty years.
He lives in the country, twenty miles from Oxford.
He always comes into town by car.

Mary Mackintosh is twenty.
She's had a lot of driving lessons. She's taken the driving test three times, but she hasn't been able to pass the test yet. She lives near the city centre, and she usually walks to work.

Bob Brewer's twenty-five.
He's been able to drive for two years, but he hasn't got a car.
He hasn't been able to save enough money.
He lives in a village outside Oxford.
He comes into Oxford by train.

Mr and Mrs Wilson are both over sixty-five.
They've never been able to drive.
They've never learned.
They live in a suburb of Oxford, and they occasionally come into town by bus.

Exercise

Mr Brown/drive/forty years.
Mr Brown's *been able to* drive *for* forty years.

Write sentences
Mary Mackintosh/not pass test/yet.
Bob Brewer/drive/two years.
Bob Brewer/not save enough money.
Mr and Mrs Wilson/never/drive.

17 Australia House

Interviewer Now, Mr. Jones . . . why do you want to go to Australia?

Mr Jones Well, I'm really thinking about my children. You see, there aren't many opportunities here. I lost my job last year and I haven't been able to find another one. Will I be able to find a job in Australia?

Interviewer What do you do?

Mr Jones I'm an electrician.

Interviewer Oh, you'll be able to find a job easily.

Mr Jones What about accommodation? Will I be able to find a house?

Interviewer Well, that is a problem . . . but there are hostels for new immigrants.

Mr Jones . . . and what about my children?

Interviewer Oh, you'll be able to find a good school in Australia.

Interviewer Now, why do you want to emigrate to Australia, Mrs Baxter?

Miss Baxter Er . . . it's Miss Baxter . . .

Interviewer Oh, I'm very sorry . . .

Miss Baxter That's all right . . . well, you see . . . I've never been able to find the right man in England . . .

Interviewer Well, Miss Baxter . . . I can't promise anything . . . but there are a lot of men in Australia . . .

Miss Baxter Will I be able to find a tall, dark, handsome man there?

Interviewer Oh, Miss Baxter . . . this is Australia House . . . not a marriage bureau!

Interviewer Come in! Take a seat . . . Mr Cook, isn't it?

Mr Cook That's right.

Interviewer Why do you want to go to Australia, Mr Cook?

Mr Cook I don't . . . I just want to leave England.

Interviewer Pardon? What qualifications have you got?

Mr Cook Qualifications? Oh, I've never been able to pass any exams.

Interviewer Well, what will you be able to do in Australia? How will you earn a living?

Mr Cook I don't know . . . but I won't be able to work very hard . . . I've got a bad back!

Look at this

He'll be able to find a job.
He won't be able to find a house.
Will she be able to find a husband?

Exercise

Complete this conversation using *be able to*.

Miss Marshall . . . a job in Australia?
Interviewer What do you do?
Miss Marshall I'm a shorthand-typist.
Interviewer Oh, . . . a job easily.

Miss Marshall What about accommodation? . . . a flat?
Interviewer Well, that's more difficult. . . . a flat immediately, but . . . one after a few months. There are hostels for new immigrants.

18 Cheques and credit

A Next, please.
B I'd like to cash this cheque, please.
A Yes, madam . . . £30. Oh! You haven't signed it yet, madam.
B Haven't I? Oh, I'm terribly sorry . . . here you are.
A Thank you. How would you like the money?
B Four fives and ten ones, please.

£30 (4 × £5/10 × £1)
£50 (5 × £10)
£100 (5 × £10/10 × £5)
£20 (2 × £5/10 × £1)

C I'd like to change these francs, please.
D Yes, sir. How many francs have you got?
C 200. What's the rate of exchange, please?
D The current rates are on the notice board, sir.

francs (200)
dollars (20)
marks (50)
yen (5000)

E I'd like to buy this . . . but I haven't got enough cash with me. Do you take travellers cheques?
F Certainly, sir.
E Good. How much is that?
F It's £30.
E What's the exchange rate?
F I'm not sure, sir . . . I'll go and check.

travellers cheques?
American dollars?
Swiss francs?
Canadian dollars?

G Good morning. Can I help you?
H Yes. My name's Davies. I'm expecting some money from my bank in Toronto.
G By post, cable, or telex, sir?
H By telex.
G Let me see. Ah, yes. Davies. £200 from the Royal Bank of Canada, Toronto. Have you got any identification, sir?
H Well, I haven't got my passport, but I've got my driving licence. Will that be all right?
G Yes, sir. That'll be all right.

Davies/£200/
Royal Bank of
Canada/Toronto

Moore/£300/
First National Bank/
Los Angeles

Butler/£100/
Bank of New South
Wales/Sydney

Kelly/£1000/
Chase Manhattan
Bank/New York

19 A holiday in Egypt

Mr Harris I looked through this brochure last night, and I'd like to book the summer holiday in Egypt.
Travel Agent Yes, sir . . . the Hotel Cleopatra?
Mr Harris That's right . . . how far is it from the hotel to the beach?
Travel Agent . . . about a two-minute walk.
Mr Harris Good. How hot is it in Egypt in July?
Travel Agent About 28°C.

Guide . . . and that's the Great Pyramid, Mr Harris.
Mr Harris Oh, yes . . . it looks very high!
Guide It's about 137 metres high.
Mr Harris How long are the sides?
Guide They're 230 metres long.
Mr Harris It's incredible! How old is it?
Guide It's nearly four and a half thousand years old.

Sailor We're going through the Suez Canal now.
Mr Harris Hmm . . . it doesn't look very wide. How wide is it?
Sailor About 60 metres . . . and it's 162 kilometres long.
Mr Harris Really? This is a big ship. How deep is the canal?
Sailor The average depth is about 10 metres . . . but they're going to make it deeper.

Guide Hello there, Mr Harris. Are you coming on the excursion to Cairo today?
Mr Harris Oh, yes! . . . How far is it?
Guide It's about 150 kilometres.
Mr Harris Good. How long will it take to get there?
Guide Only three hours.

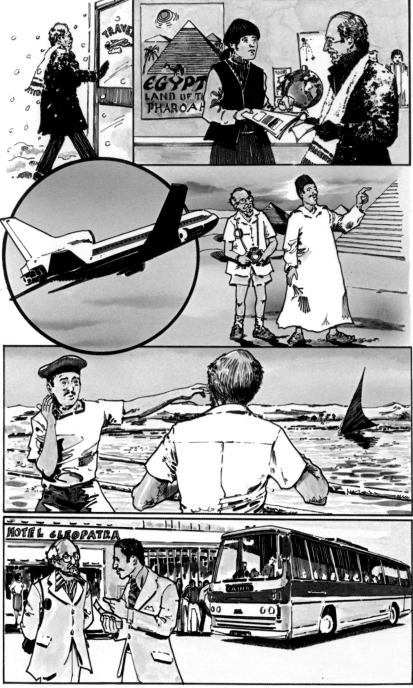

Exercise 1

How far is it?

	Birmingham	Bristol	Glasgow	Leeds	Manchester	Southampton
Bristol	87					
Glasgow	287	365				
Leeds	109	194	210			
Manchester	79	159	211	40		
Southampton	128	75	415	224	206	
London	110	116	392	190	184	77

How far is it from Birmingham to Bristol?
It's eighty-seven miles.
Write six sentences like this.

Exercise 2

Maria
1m 90cm
Age: 30
Weight: 75 kilos

Hans
1m 85cm
Age: 42
Weight: 65 kilos

How old is Maria?
She's thirty.
How tall is she?
She's 1 m 90 cm tall.
How heavy is she?
She's 75 kilos.

Write three questions about Hans.

20 Comparisons

Mr and Mrs Kent are old age pensioners. They go to the shops every Saturday. They have to walk up a very steep hill between their house and the shops. They both walk slowly. Mr Kent always has to wait for his wife at the top of the hill, because Mrs Kent walks more slowly than Mr Kent.

Diana and Margaret work in the same office. They're both good typists because they type carefully. Diana never makes a mistake and Margaret rarely makes a mistake. Diana types more carefully than Margaret.

Some drivers occasionally have accidents, but Alan and David are very careless drivers. Alan has already had two accidents this year, and David has had a lot. David drives even more carelessly than Alan.

Both Carlos and Miguel are good students. They speak English well, but Miguel has spent a year in England, so he speaks English better than Carlos.

Tyneside United and Humber Rovers are both near the bottom of the Fourth Division. The football season has nearly finished, and Tyneside have won only one match. They've played very badly. Humber Rovers haven't won a match yet, and they haven't scored a goal. Humber have played even worse than Tyneside.

DIVISION FOUR	played	won	lost	drawn	points	position
Mersey Town	43	7	30	6	20	**21**
Thamesford	42	3	29	10	16	**22**
Tyneside United	43	1	35	7	9	**23**
Humber Rovers	43	0	41	2	2	24

Tony and Jim work for a construction company. They're very hard workers. They work about twelve hours a day. Tony often works at weekends. He earns more money than Jim because he works harder than Jim.

Look at this

slowly	more slowly
carefully	more carefully
dangerously	more dangerously
well	better
badly	worse
hard	harder
fast	faster

21 A day off work

Bill Walker works for an import-export company. Last Wednesday morning Bill rang his office at nine o'clock. His boss, Mr Thompson, answered the phone.

Mr Thompson Hello, Thompson here . . .
Bill Hello. This is Bill Walker.
Mr Thompson Oh, hello, Bill.
Bill I'm afraid I can't come to work today, Mr Thompson.
Mr Thompson Oh, what's the problem?
Bill I've got a very sore throat.
Mr Thompson Yes, you sound ill on the phone.
Bill Yes, I'll stay in bed today, but I'll be able to come tomorrow.
Mr Thompson That's all right, Bill. Stay in bed until you feel well enough to work.
Bill Thank you, Mr Thompson. . . . Goodbye.
Mr Thompson Goodbye, Bill.

Mr Thompson liked Bill very much. At 12.30 he got into his car, drove to a shop and bought some fruit for him. He went to Bill's flat and rang the doorbell. Bill's wife, Susan, answered the door.

Susan Oh, Mr Thompson! Hello . . . how are you?
Mr Thompson Fine, thanks, Susan. I've just come to see Bill. How is he?
Susan He doesn't look very well. I wanted him to see the doctor.
Mr Thompson I'll go in and see him. . . . Hello, Bill!
Bill Oh . . . hello . . . hello, Mr Thompson . . . er . . . er . . .
Mr Thompson I've brought some fruit for you, Bill.
Bill Thank you very much, Mr Thompson.
Mr Thompson Well . . . I had to pass your house anyway. How's your throat?
Bill It seems a little better. I'll be O.K. tomorrow.
Mr Thompson Well, don't come in until you feel better.
Bill All right . . . but I'm sure I'll be able to come in tomorrow.
Mr Thompson Goodbye, Bill.
Bill Goodbye, Mr Thompson.

At three o'clock in the afternoon, Mr Thompson locked his office door, and switched on his portable television. He wanted to watch an important international football match. It was England against Brazil. Both teams were playing well, but neither team could score a goal. The crowd were cheering and booing. It was very exciting.

Then at 3.20, England scored from a penalty. Mr Thompson jumped out of his chair. He was very excited. He was smiling happily when suddenly the cameraman focussed on the crowd. Mr Thompson's smile disappeared and he looked very angry. Bill Walker's face, in close-up, was there on the screen. He didn't look ill, and he didn't sound ill. He was smiling happily and cheering wildly!

22 Applying for a job

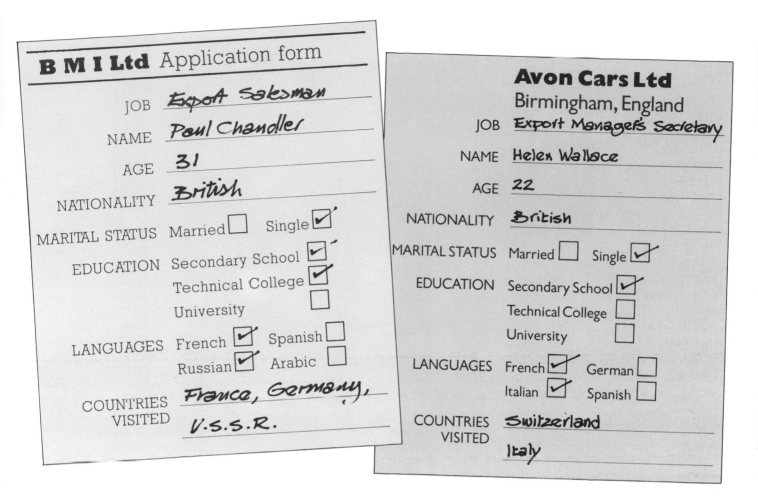

B M I Ltd Application form

JOB _Export Salesman_
NAME _Paul Chandler_
AGE _31_
NATIONALITY _British_
MARITAL STATUS Married ☐ Single ☑
EDUCATION Secondary School ☑
Technical College ☑
University ☐
LANGUAGES French ☑ Spanish ☐
Russian ☑ Arabic ☐
COUNTRIES VISITED _France, Germany, U.S.S.R._

Avon Cars Ltd
Birmingham, England
JOB _Export Manager's Secretary_
NAME _Helen Wallace_
AGE _22_
NATIONALITY _British_
MARITAL STATUS Married ☐ Single ☑
EDUCATION Secondary School ☑
Technical College ☐
University ☐
LANGUAGES French ☑ German ☐
Italian ☑ Spanish ☐
COUNTRIES VISITED _Switzerland_ _Italy_

Interviewer Come in . . . come in. It's Mr Chandler, isn't it?
Mr Chandler Yes, that's right. How do you do?
Interviewer How do you do? Please take a seat.
Mr Chandler Thank you very much.
Interviewer Well, I've got your application form here. I just want to check the information . . . is that all right?
Mr Chandler Yes, of course.
Interviewer Now, you're 31, aren't you?
Mr Chandler Yes, I am.
Interviewer . . . and you aren't married, are you?
Mr Chandler No, I'm not . . . not yet.
Interviewer Uh, huh. You went to secondary school and technical college, didn't you?
Mr Chandler Yes, I did.
Interviewer . . . but you didn't go to university, did you?
Mr Chandler No, I didn't. I started work when I was 20.
Interviewer I see. You can speak French and Russian, can't you?
Mr Chandler Yes, I can . . . but not fluently. I speak French better than Russian.
Interviewer . . . but you can't speak Spanish, can you?
Mr Chandler No, no, I can't.
Interviewer You've been to France, haven't you?
Mr Chandler Yes, I have . . . and to Germany and Russia.
Interviewer So I see . . . but you haven't been to the Middle East, have you?
Mr Chandler No, I'm afraid I haven't, but I'd like to.
Interviewer Good.

Fill in the spaces

Interviewer Come in. Please sit down. It's Miss Wallace, . . . ?
Miss Wallace Yes, that's right. Good afternoon.
Interviewer Good afternoon. Well, I've looked through your application. Can I just check the information?
Miss Wallace Of course.
Interviewer Now, you're 22, . . . ?
Miss Wallace Yes, I am.
Interviewer You aren't married, . . . ?
Miss Wallace No, I'm not, but I'm engaged.
Interviewer You didn't go to technical college or university, . . . ?
Miss Wallace No, I didn't.
Interviewer But you learned to type at secondary school, . . . ?
Miss Wallace Yes, I did.
Interviewer You can speak French and Italian, . . . ?
Miss Wallace Yes, I can, but I can write them better than I can speak them.
Interviewer I see. You've been to Switzerland, . . . ?
Miss Wallace Yes, I have. And Italy.
Interviewer And you can take shorthand, . . . ?
Miss Wallace Yes, I studied it at school.

23 Four disasters

Good evening. Our programme tonight is about disasters. This year there have been fires, plane crashes, earthquakes, and volcanic eruptions. All our guests tonight have survived disasters.

Hi! I'm Bill Daniels. I live in Chicago. I was working in my office on the 28th floor of a skyscraper. I was dictating some letters to my secretary when the fire-bell rang. I rushed out to the lift but it wasn't working. The stairs were full of thick smoke. We couldn't go down, so we had to go up to the roof. When we got there some people were waiting calmly. Others were shouting and screaming wildly. A helicopter managed to land on the roof and rescued six of us before the building collapsed.

My name's Martha Huggins. I was on holiday in the South Pacific and I was staying on Pogohiti, a small island. I was having a rest when the volcano erupted. The noise woke me up. I looked through the window. Everybody was running towards the harbour. I just put on a coat, and ran to the harbour too. I managed to get on a ship. It was leaving when the lava hit the town.

Hello, I'm George Green. I'm a farmer. I was working in the field behind my house when I saw the plane. It was on fire. Smoke was coming from the engines, and it was coming down fast. I was running towards my house when it crashed into the trees behind me. I heard a terrible explosion . . . when I woke up, I was lying in a hospital bed.

Good evening. My name's Michael Purt. My wife and I were staying with friends on Santa Monica in the Caribbean. We were having dinner when the earthquake began. Everything shook. All the plates and food fell onto the floor. We were picking everything up when the ceiling fell onto us. We couldn't move, and we had to wait for three hours before help arrived.

24 A letter from Paris

John lives in Manchester. His girlfriend, Mary, is studying French in Paris. She's been there for five weeks. He wants to visit her in Paris and he wrote to her about it last week. He's just received this reply from her.

68 rue des Alpes,
Paris.
September 9th

Dear John,

Thanks for your letter. I'm sorry I haven't been able to write for two weeks, but I've had to do a lot of homework. My exams will be in four weeks and I can't speak French well enough yet.

I'm very glad you want to come to Paris. Will you be able to come soon? I want to show you everything, and I want you to meet all my friends. I've made a lot of friends since I came here. You'll have to speak French because some of them can't speak English very well. It won't be too difficult for you, will it? You studied French at school, didn't you?

How long will you be able to stay? I've been able to find a little studio flat. The address is at the top of the letter. It wasn't easy to find. Flats are difficult to find in Paris. I'll be able to cook a real French dinner for you! I had to get a flat because the hotel was too expensive for me.

Write to me soon.
Lots of love,
Mary.

Mr. John C__
13 Nels__
Mos__

Look at this example

Thanks/letter. I/sorry/not write/a long time.
Thanks for your letter. I'm sorry I haven't been able to write for a long time.

Now, use these words and write a letter:

Thanks/letter. I/sorry/not write/a long time. I/study/every night.
My test/two weeks, and I/English/yet.
I/happy/you/come/England. You/soon? I/show/a
lot of interesting places. I/you/meet/English friends. I/lot/since/here.
You/English because/none/(Spanish). It/too difficult?
You/English/school? How long/stay? I/find/flat.
Address/top/letter. Flats/difficult/England.
I/cook/good English dinner. I/flat/hotel/expensive/me.

25 Travelling by air

A Can I check in here for the British Airways flight to New York?

B Yes, sir. May I see your ticket, and your passport?

A Here you are.

B That's fine. Can you put your suitcase on the scales, please?

A Of course. How much does it weigh?

B 23 kilos. I'm sorry, but you'll have to pay an excess baggage charge.

A Oh! It's only three kilos overweight.

B Yes, sir . . . that's £6. . . . Thank you. Would you like to go through to the departure lounge?

British Airways/ New York
Air France/Paris
T.W.A./San Francisco
British Caledonian/ Athens

23 kilos/3 kilos/£6
21 kilos/1 kilo/£2
30 kilos/10 kilos/£20
25 kilos/5 kilos/£10

('British Airways Flight 179 to New York is now boarding at Gate 4')

A Excuse me . . . .

C Yes?

A I didn't hear that announcement. Which flight did they call?

C Flight 179 to New York . . . are you going there?

A Yes.

C So am I . . . Gate 4's this way . . . follow me!

Flight 179/
New York/
Gate 4

Flight 236/
Paris/
Gate 13

Flight 784/
San Francisco/
Gate 11

Flight 119/
Athens/
Gate 3

D May I search you, sir? It's just a security check.

A Of course.

D Thank you. Oh, what's this in your pocket?

A Oh, yes . . . I'm sorry. It's just a metal comb.

D Hmm . . . May I see it, sir?

A Certainly . . . here it is.

a metal comb
a cigarette case
my car keys
a penknife

'Good afternoon, ladies and gentlemen. Captain Gibson and his crew welcome you aboard British Airways Flight 179 to New York. We're now flying at a height of 30,000 feet. Our speed is approximately 600 miles an hour. We'll land in New York in five and a half hours. The temperature in New York is now minus 3°C. In a few minutes you'll be able to see the Irish Coast. Our stewards and stewardesses will serve lunch in half an hour.'

Height: 30,000 feet
35,000 feet
25,000 feet

Speed: 600 mph
620 mph
550 mph

Temperature: −3°C
10°C
25°C

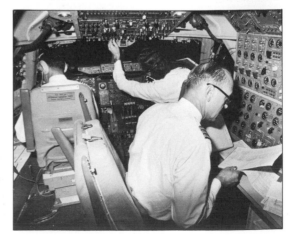

26 I've cut myself!

A Ow! This knife's sharp! I've cut myself.
B Let me see it . . . oh, it's O.K. You haven't cut yourself badly . . . it's only a scratch.
A But my finger's bleeding!
B Don't be a baby! It isn't bleeding much. I'll get a bandage.

C Did you see the play on television last night?
D No, I didn't. What was it?
C *Romeo and Juliet*. I cried.
D Cried? Why?
C Well, it was very sad. At the end, Romeo killed himself and then Juliet killed herself.
D It sounds silly to me! Why did they kill themselves?
C . . . for love!
D Oh! They were silly, weren't they?

E Now, my guests tonight are the two rock musicians, Dean and Darren Osborne.
F Hello!
E Now, you both play the guitar very well. Did anyone teach you?
F No . . . we just bought some guitars and we taught ourselves.
E I see.

G Sorry, I'm late . . .
H Oh, that's all right, Mrs Green.
G It was our first wedding anniversary yesterday.
H Oh, congratulations!
G Thank you. We went to that new restaurant in the High Street.
H Did you enjoy yourselves?
G Oh yes, we had a very good time. We had two bottles of champagne!

I Have you seen my new electric cooker?
J No, I haven't.
I Oh, it's wonderful. It's got an automatic timer. It can switch itself on and off.

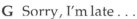

Exercise

I've cut *myself*.

1 She's holding a mirror. She's looking at . . . .
2 Be careful, John! Don't hurt . . . !
3 He taught . . . to play the guitar.
4 Romeo and Juliet killed . . . .
5 We went to a party last night. We enjoyed . . . very much.
6 My washing machine is automatic. It switches . . . off.
7 They're enjoying . . . . They're on holiday.

27 Choosing a pet

Shop Assistant Good afternoon, madam. Can I help you?

Customer Yes. I'm looking for a pet for my son. Can you suggest anything?

Assistant What kind of pet does he want? A traditional pet . . . a cat . . . or a dog? Or something unusual?

Customer Well, he'd like a snake or a crocodile, but he isn't going to get one.

Assistant We've got a nice Alsatian dog at the moment.

Customer An Alsatian? Did you say 'an Alsatian'? Oh no, I've read about them in the paper. They're very big and savage.

Assistant Oh, no, madam. They aren't as savage as some dogs.

Customer Really?

Assistant Oh, yes. Last week we had a small dog. It was only as big as your handbag, but it was as savage as a tiger . . . it bit me three times!

Customer Perhaps not a dog, then.

Assistant How about a cat?

Customer A cat? Hmm . . . they aren't as friendly as dogs, are they?

Assistant No, but they don't eat as much as dogs either. And they're very clean. They wash themselves every day.

Customer Hmm . . .

Assistant Or how about a bird? A parrot or a budgie? We've got both.

Customer Which do you recommend?

Assistant Well, budgies aren't as easy to train and they never speak as well as parrots.

Customer Yes, but budgies don't need as much space as parrots, do they?

Assistant That's true. Budgies are very popular because they're so easy to keep.

Customer Yes . . . but they're a bit noisy, aren't they? I want a quiet pet.

Assistant A quiet pet? Well, how about a goldfish? There's nothing as quiet as a goldfish.

1

Mick/Jack/strong
Mick is as strong as Jack.

whisky/gin/expensive

today/yesterday/wet

the skyscraper/the church/high

this sack/that sack/heavy

2

Her hair/his hair/long
Her hair isn't as long as his hair.

portable typewriters/electric typewriters/good

English/Chinese/difficult

my writing/her writing/clear

motorways/country roads/interesting

3

work hard/your boss
Do you work as hard as your boss?

drive fast/James Hunt

type carefully/Elizabeth

speak well/the teacher

dance beautifully/Anne

4

Jumbo jets/Concorde/high
Jumbo jets don't fly as high as Concordes

Fred/Ian/hard

Mike/John/well

Sam/Bill/carefully

Frank/Rockie/loudly

5

Tom/drunk/wine/Robert
Tom hasn't drunk as much wine as Robert.

Tom/smoked/cigarettes/Robert
Tom hasn't smoked as many cigarettes as Robert.

Humber/scored/goals/Tyneside

Tom/spent/money/Robert

Ron/caught/fish/Bob

Mrs Jones/bought/food/Mrs Smith

DAILY NEWS

8p

WEDNESDAY, JUNE 20th

No. 712 142

£5,000 BANK ROBBERY IN THE CITY

There was a bank robbery in central London yesterday. Just before closing time yesterday, a man entered the Butcher Street Branch of the National Westminster Bank. He was carrying a shotgun, and wearing a stocking mask over his head. There were only a few customers in the bank at the time. He made them lie on the floor, and forced the cashier to put the money in a sack. As he was leaving, the security guard tried to ring the alarm. The robber shot him and the guard is now in St Patrick's Hospital. Surgeons are trying to save his life. Last night the police arrested a man in South London. He is now helping the police with their enquiries.

STATEMENT OF WITNESS
(C.J. Act 1967, ss. 2, 9; M.C. Rules 1968, r.58)

STATEMENT OF .... John Alfred Smithers ....

(Full Name)

AGE .... 36 .... OCCUPATION .... Car Salesman ....

ADDRESS .... Flat 4., Paradise Court, Ealing, London. W5.

This statement (consisting of **one** pages each signed by me), is true to the best of my knowledge and belief and I make it knowing that, if it is tendered in evidence, I shall be liable to prosecution if I have wilfully stated in it anything which I know to be false or do not believe to be true.

On Tuesday afternoon I was at Ascot races with my girlfriend, Isadora Bell. We left my flat at 1 o'clock in my white Jaguar and drove to Ascot. We didn't stop for petrol but we had lunch in a pub. I don't remember the name of the pub, but it was somewhere between London and Ascot. We had beer and sandwiches outside. We arrived at the race-track at 1.55, in time for the first race. We stayed there until the last race at 5 o'clock. We were very lucky. I won a lot of money but I can't remember exactly how much. That's why I had a lot of money in my flat when the police came to my flat at 6.00. I left Isadora in Central London. She wanted to buy some clothes in Oxford Street. I don't know where she is now.

Signed .... John A. Smithers ....
20·6·79

Statement taken and signature witnessed by .... D. Cooper ....
Rank and Number .... P.C. 3249 .....

GEN 6 (2/77)

An interrogation . . .

Now, put in the correct question tags:
    You're John Alfred Smithers, *aren't you*?

Police Constable You're John Alfred
    Smithers, . . . ?
Smithers Yes, I am.
PC You're 36, . . . ?
S Yes, that's right. It was my birthday
    yesterday.
PC You sell cars, . . . ?
S Yes, I do. And other things.
PC You live in Ealing, . . . ?
S Yes, I do. I've lived here all my life.
PC You went to Ascot races yesterday,
    . . . ?
S That's right.
PC You weren't alone, . . . ?
S No, I wasn't. I was with Isadora Bell.
PC But you're married, . . . , Smithers?
S Yes, but I haven't seen my wife
    for three years.
PC I see. Now you left your flat at one
    o'clock, . . . ?
S Yes. About one o'clock.
PC You were in your Jaguar, . . . ?
S Yes, I was.
PC You didn't stop for petrol, . . . ?
S No.
PC You had lunch in an Indian
    restaurant, . . . ?
S Oh, no we didn't. We had lunch in a
    pub.
PC You don't remember the name of the
    pub, . . . ?
S No, I'm afraid I don't.
PC You had chicken and chips, . . . ?
S No, no, no. We had beer and
    sandwiches outside.
PC You arrived in time for the first race,
    and stayed until the last race, . . . ?
S Yes!
PC You were very lucky, . . . ?
S Yes, I was.
PC You won £5,000, . . . ?
S No, I can't remember exactly how
    much.
PC There was £5,000 in your flat, . . . ?
S Was there?
PC You don't know where Miss Bell is
    now, . . . ?
S No, I'm not her husband, . . . ?
PC But you left her in Central London,
    because she wanted to buy some
    clothes.
S Yes, yes.
PC It's very interesting, . . . , Mr
    Smithers. You've got a very fast car,
    . . . ?
S What do you mean?

The last race at Ascot began late and it didn't finish until twenty-five past five, so you drove from Ascot to Central London and back to Ealing in 35 minutes, in the rush hour. That's impossible, . . . Mr Smithers!

29 Dinner with friends

Ken Hello!

Rob Hello, Ken . . . Hello, Barbara. Come in. Shall I take your coats?

Ken Oh, thank you very much. What a lovely house!

Rob I'm glad you like it. Dinner's nearly ready.

Ken Where's Anna?

Rob Oh, she's in the kitchen. She'll be here in a minute. Just go into the dining-room. How about a drink before dinner?

Ken That's a nice idea!

kitchen
 . . . dining room
bathroom
 . . . lounge
bedroom
 . . . living room
baby's room
 . . . dining room

Anna Here we are . . . dinner's ready. Sit down everybody!

Barbara Thank you very much, Anna. Everything looks wonderful, and it smells delicious, too.

Anna I'll put the salad in the middle of the table. Shall I serve you?

Barbara No, it's all right. We can help ourselves.

Anna Rob, could you pour the wine, please? Ken, help yourself to vegetables, too.

salad
 middle of the table
vegetables
 over here
potatoes
 at the end of the table
peas
 next to you

Rob Would you like some more brandy, Barbara?

Barbara Oh, no thanks . . . no more for me. I'm driving tonight.

Rob Oh, come on . . . just a small one.

Barbara No, really . . . I mustn't. I'll help Anna with the washing-up.

Rob The washing-up! No, no, don't worry. We always leave that until the morning.

brandy
whisky
wine
liqueur

Rob Here are your coats.

Ken Thanks . . . it's been a marvellous evening. It was very kind of you to invite us.

Rob Don't mention it . . . it was nice to see you again.

Ken Well, we enjoyed ourselves very much.

Rob I'm glad . . . you must come again.

Ken Goodnight . . . and thanks again.

Rob Goodnight . . . and drive carefully. It's a very wet night.

wet
foggy
windy
frosty
misty

30 The bad boy of British football

Stanley Walsh, the Eastfield United football star, is in the news again. Yesterday he didn't arrive for a training session. Last night, Brian Huff, Eastfield's manager, was very angry. Stanley has had a lot of arguments with Huff. Huff spoke to our reporter last night.

Our reporter later spoke to Mrs Lucy Walsh in her £50,000 apartment.

Our reporter found Stanley at his villa in Spain. He was with Inger Carlson, the Swedish actress. He seemed very happy.

R Where is Stanley, Mr Huff?
H We don't know.
R When did you last see him?
H We spoke to each other five days ago. I haven't seen him since then.
R How angry are you?
H Very. This is the end. Stanley Walsh won't play for us again.
R But Stanley's the best player in England, isn't he? Did he give a reason?
H No, he didn't.
R Has Stanley got any personal problems, Mr Huff?
H I don't know . . . but he's a very selfish man. He only thinks about himself.

R Where is Stanley, Mrs Walsh?
L I don't know and I don't care.
R When did you last see him?
L We haven't seen each other for two weeks.
R Have you spoken to each other . . . or written to each other recently?
L No. We never want to see each other again.
R But why, Mrs Walsh?
L Ask Stanley!

R How long have you known each other, Stanley?
S We met each other in a disco three weeks ago. It was love at first sight.
R But what about your football?
S Oh, football can wait. Inger's the most important thing in my life. We love each other very much and we understand each other.
R And your wife, Stanley? What about your wife?
S Oh, that finished a long time ago.
R What happened?
S Well, I was in love with Lucy for a long time. We taught each other a lot, but . . .
R But what?
S Well, we started to hate each other. We couldn't even look at each other.
R So, what are you going to do next?
S I don't know. . . . Ask Inger!

Exercise
Look at this:
I haven't spoken to her. She hasn't spoken to me.
We haven't spoken to each other.

He met her. She met him.
They met each other.

Now you do the same:

1 I love her. She loves me.
2 He's seen her. She's seen him.
3 He needs her. She needs him.
4 I wrote to him. He wrote to me.
5 I've helped him. He's helped me.

31 So am I!

A I'm on holiday next month.
B So am I.
A I need a change.
B Oh, so do I. I'm tired of the same office and the same people every day!
A Where are you going?
B Spain.
A Oh, I went there last year.
B So did I. We always go to Spain . . . but we never go to the Costa Brava.
A No, neither do I. There are too many English people there.
B Where exactly are you going?
A San Pedro . . . it's a little village on the north coast.
B You're joking!
A No, I'm not. I've been there three times.
B So have we . . . and we're going there this year, too.
A . . . not to the Hotel del Sol?
B Yes . . . why?
A Well, I'll see you. I'm staying there too!

1 A I'm happy.
  B So am I.
  A I'm not crazy.
  B Neither am I.

2 A I'm not a student.
  B I am.
  A I'm a teacher.
  B I'm not.

3 A I've got a book.
  B So have I.
  A I haven't got a Rolls-Royce.
  B Neither have I.

4 A I haven't got any money.
  B I have.
  A I've got an electronic watch.
  B I haven't.

5 A I like music.
  B So do I.
  A I don't like snakes.
  B Neither do I.

6 A I don't eat meat.
  B I do.
  A I come to school on Sundays.
  B I don't.

7 A I was here last week.
  B So was I.
  A I wasn't late this morning.
  B Neither was I.

8 A I wasn't at home yesterday evening.
  B I was.
  A I was at the cinema last night.
  B I wasn't.

9 A I studied mathematics at school.
  B So did I.
  A I didn't go to the cinema last night.
  B Neither did I.

10 A I didn't play sports at school.
  B I did.
  A I had wine with dinner last night.
  B I didn't.

32 A family problem

Flat 4
185 Kings Road
Chelsea
London S.W.3
5th May 1979

Dear Daddy,

Thank you very much for the birthday present. I was very pleased with the Ferrari, but I didn't like the colour, so I'm going to change it.

I saw Tom again yesterday. You're worried about him, aren't you? Well, don't worry about *him*. He's all right. He's very good at his job ... he's a drummer in a pop group. I'm going to bring him for dinner next weekend, so you can meet him.

Love,
Samantha

P.S. We love each other very much. He isn't interested in your money.

Worth House,
Mansford, Hampshire.

15th May 1979

Dear Samantha,

I'm sorry about last weekend. I was very angry with Tom, but he was very rude to me. I'm not a stupid old fool. I'm tired of long-haired young men! He didn't even dress for dinner! You love him, I know.

I just feel sorry for you, and I'm worried about your future. Tom likes pop music. He isn't interested in anything else. He isn't interested in you at all. You're making a terrible mistake. And I'm glad he isn't interested in my money, because he isn't going to get any.

Love,

Daddy.

Exercise

I'm interested in politics.
What are you interested in?
I'm good at English, but I'm bad at mathematics.
What about you?
I'm worried about money.
What about you?
I'm tired of this town.
What about you?
I'm very pleased with your English.
What about you?

Good evening! I'm Martin Smiles. Welcome to the 'Yes/No Contest'. Now, the rules are very simple. I'm going to ask questions for 30 seconds. You mustn't answer with 'Yes' or 'No', and you mustn't nod or shake your head. Well, here's our first contestant . . .Mrs Alice Leach from Nottingham.

Smiles What's your name?
Mrs Leach Alice . . . Alice Leach.
Smiles Where are you from, Alice?
Mrs Leach Nottingham.
Smiles Did you say 'Birmingham'?
Mrs Leach No, Notting . . . (*dong*)
Smiles Oh, dear. I am sorry, Mrs Leach. Now our next contestant is Ralph Milton, from Blackpool. It's Mr Milton, isn't it?
Milton That's right.
Smiles Good . . . you aren't nervous, are you?
Milton I'm not nervous.
Smiles Did you shake your head?
Milton I didn't.
Smiles Are you sure?
Milton Yes . . . (*dong*)
Smiles Oh . . . I'm dreadfully sorry. Better luck next time, Mr Milton. Now, here's our third contestant. It's Brian Tankard from Bristol. Hello, Brian.
Brian Hello.
Smiles You work in a bank, don't you?
Brian That's correct.
Smiles Do you like your job?
Brian I enjoy it very much.
Smiles Oh, do you?
Brian I said 'I enjoy it very much.'
Smiles Now, you aren't married, are you?
Brian I am married.
Smiles Is your wife here tonight?
Brian She's at home.
Smiles So she isn't here.
Brian Of course not.
Smiles Have you got any children?
Brian I've got two children.
Smiles Two boys?
Brian A boy and a girl.
Smiles and . . . (*ding*). That's 30 seconds. Well done! You've done it! Isn't that wonderful, everybody? He's won tonight's star prize . . . a brand new fully automatic dishwasher!

Look at these expressions

Yes	No	
That's right	That's wrong	
That's correct	That isn't correct	I don't know
Of course	Of course not	I'm not sure
That's true	That isn't true	I'm not certain
I agree	I disagree	

Practice

Now play the 'Yes/No Contest' with other people in your class

34 I used to . . .

A Tom! You never talk to me nowadays.
B What did you say?
A . . . and you never listen to me, either.
B Pardon?
A You used to take me out, you used to buy me presents, and you used to remember my birthday.
B But I always remember your birthday, darling.
A Do you? Well, it was yesterday! I'm going home to mother!

C Dorchester 17908 . . .
D Hello, Angela?
C Oh, hello, Mum.
D How's the baby today?
C Oh, he's crying again. He cries all day.
D You can't complain! When you were a baby, you used to cry all day and all night!
C Oh, I know, Mum . . . but I feel so tired . . . there's so much housework.
D But you've got a washing machine, a tumble dryer, a vacuum-cleaner and a dishwasher . . . I used to do everything by hand.
C I know, I know . . . I've heard all this before!
D I'm sorry, dear . . . I'll come and help you.

E Stanley, you used to be the best footballer in England. Are you going to come back and play again?
F Oh, no . . . no, I'm not.
E Why not?
F Well, football used to be the most important thing in my life . . . but it isn't any more. For ten years I used to practise every day. I never used to smoke, drink, or stay up late.
E Why has your life changed, Stanley?
F Well, I was poor then, but I'm not now. I don't need to play football any more!

G Dad?
H Yes . . .
G There's a good film on in town.
H Oh, yes . . . what is it?
G *War in Space*.
H Are you going to see it?
G I'd like to . . . all my friends are going . . . but I haven't got any money.
H All right, all right. How much do you want?
G Three pounds.
H Three pounds! When I was your age, I only used to pay five pence for the cinema.
G That was a long time ago, Dad.
H Yes, but my father used to earn three pounds for a week's work!

Exercise

I used to eat a lot of sweets when I was young, but I don't any more.
What about you?
What did you use to do when you were young, that you don't do any more?

Write four sentences.

35 A busy office

Mr Power Yes, Miss Wright? What is it?
Miss Wright Mr Hudson wants to speak
to you, sir.
Mr Power I'm very busy at the moment.
Ask him to ring later.
Miss Wright Yes, sir.
Mr Power Oh, and Miss Wright? Tell
Chris to photocopy the Director's
report.
Miss Wright Yes, sir. Anything else, sir?
Mr Power Yes. Tell Miss Davis not to
ring her boyfriend on the office phone.
Miss Wright Yes, sir.

Hello? This is Mr Power's secretary . . .
Mr Hudson Yes . . . Hudson, here.
Miss Wright I'm afraid Mr Power's busy
at the moment. Can you ring later?
Mr Hudson All right . . . what about this
afternoon?
Miss Wright Yes, that'll be all right.

Miss Wright Oh, Chris?
Chris Yes, Miss Wright?
Miss Wright Mr Power wants you to
photocopy this report.
Chris Oh, yes . . . I'll do it later.
Miss Wright No, Chris . . . do it now . . . I
know it's important.

Miss Wright Miss Davis! Did you ring
your boyfriend on the office phone
yesterday?
Miss Davis Well, yes . . . I did . . . but it
was urgent.
Miss Wright Hmm . . . I think Mr Power
heard you. He wasn't very pleased
about it. Don't use the office phone for
personal calls.
Miss Davis No . . . no, Miss Wright . . . I
won't do it again . . . I'm sorry.

Mr Power Miss Wright? Did you speak
to Mr Hudson?
Miss Wright Yes, I did. I asked him to
ring later. He says he'll ring you this
afternoon.
Mr Power That's fine. Has Chris photo-
copied that report yet?
Miss Wright Not yet . . . but I told him to
do it immediately. I think he's doing it
now.
Mr Power Good. Did you tell Miss Davis
not to ring her boyfriend from here?
Miss Wright Oh, yes . . . I told her not to
use the office phone for personal calls
. . . she says she won't do it again. I'm
sure she won't.
Mr Power I hope she won't . . . her
boyfriend lives in Australia!

Look at this

"Ask him to ring later."
"Can you ring later?"
She asked him to ring later.

"Tell her not to use the telephone."
"Please don't use the telephone."
She told her not to use the telephone.

Exercise

"I can't do it." (he says)
He says he can't do it.

1 "That'll be all right." (she thinks)
2 "It's important." (she knows)
3 "I'm busy." (he's afraid)
4 "She won't do it again." (she's sure)
5 "She rang her boyfriend." (she's sorry)
6 "Her boyfriend lives in Australia." (he says)

36 The smuggler

Sam Lewis was a customs officer. He used to work in a small border town. It wasn't a busy town and there wasn't much work. The road was usually very quiet and there weren't many travellers. It wasn't a very interesting job, but Sam liked an easy life. About once a week, he used to meet an old man. His name was Draper. He always used to arrive at the border early in the morning in a big truck. The truck was always empty. After a while Sam became suspicious. He often used to search the truck, but he never found anything. One day he asked Draper about his job. Draper laughed and said, 'I'm a smuggler.'

Last year Sam retired. He spent his savings on an expensive holiday. He flew to Bermuda, and stayed in a luxury hotel. One day, he was sitting by the pool and opposite him he saw Draper drinking champagne. Sam walked over to him.

Sam Hello, there!
Draper Hi!
Sam Do you remember me?
Draper Yes . . . of course I do. You're a customs officer.
Sam I used to be, but I'm not any more. I retired last month. I often used to search your truck . . .
Draper . . . but you never found anything!
Sam No, I didn't. Can I ask you something?
Draper Of course you can.
Sam Were you a smuggler?
Draper Of course I was.
Sam But . . . the truck was always empty. What were you smuggling?
Draper Trucks!

37 I'm bored

Jim I'm bored.
Jean Well . . . do something interesting.
Jim What, for example?
Jean Go to the cinema.
Jim The cinema bores me.
Jean Always?
Jim Yes. All the films are so boring. I'm not interested in sex and violence.
Jean Well, what interests you then?
Jim Nothing!
Jean You need some fresh air!

Helen Have you heard the news, Bill?
Bill No, why?
Helen A war has just started in Mandanga.
Bill Mandanga? Where's that?
Helen I don't know exactly . . . but it's worrying. They showed a television report last night.
Bill Well, I'm not worried about it. I never watch the news these days. I prefer sports programmes.
Helen Why aren't you interested in the news?
Bill Well, all the news is bad. I just want entertainment in the evenings.

Peter What are you doing tonight, Mike?
Mike I'm staying in. There's a good horror film on the 'telly'.
Peter What is it?
Mike *The Blood of Frankenstein.*
Peter Oh, that sounds frightening.
Mike Not really . . . I think horror films are amusing.
Peter Amusing? Horror films?
Mike Yes. I went with Anne to see *Dracula* last week. I was very amused. I laughed from beginning to end.
Peter What about Anne?
Mike Oh, she was terrified. She was under the seat.

Nick Did you go to the football match on Saturday?
Ben Yes, I did.
Nick It was very exciting, wasn't it?
Ben Yes it was. Both teams attacked.
Nick Yes. 1-0 . . . 1-1 . . . 2-1 . . . 2-2 . . . 2-3 . . . 3-3 . . .
Ben My brother was so excited near the end that he threw his hat in the air when Manchester scored their fourth goal.
Nick Did he find his hat?
Ben Yes, but it was a bit embarrassing. He had to ask a policeman for it.

Look at this

I'm bored	it's boring	it bores me
He's interested	it's interesting	it interests him
She's worried	it's worrying	it worries her
We're frightened	it's frightening	it frightens us
You're amused	it's amusing	it amuses you
They're terrified	it's terrifying	it terrifies them
I'm excited	it's exciting	it excites me
He's embarrassed	it's embarrassing	it embarrasses him

38 Advice

Andrea What's the matter, Jenny? You look worried.

Jenny Yes . . . I'm trying to lose weight.

Andrea Oh, you don't need to lose weight.

Jenny Oh, I do! I've just bought some new jeans and I can't get them on. They're too tight.

Andrea Well, you should go on a diet.

Jenny I know, but what kind of diet?

Andrea You should eat lots of salad and fruit.

Jenny Yes, but I don't like salad . . . I prefer meat.

Andrea Well, you can eat meat, but you shouldn't eat too much. You shouldn't eat bread or potatoes, either.

Jenny What about alcohol? Can I drink wine?

Andrea Oh, no, you should never drink alcohol.

Max What's the matter, Peter? You don't look very happy.

Peter I'm not. I'm worried about my English.

Max What's the problem?

Peter I'm not practising enough.

Max Why not?

Peter Well, it's difficult to meet English people.

Max You should go out more.

Peter Where should I go?

Max You should go to pubs, you should join a club.

Peter But . . . English people never speak to me.

Max Ah! You should speak first.

Peter What can I talk about?

Max The weather! English people are always interested in the weather!

Wendy Hello, Charles . . . you look tired today.

Charles Yes, I'm working too hard.

Wendy You should take a holiday.

Charles Yes, I know I should . . . but we're just too busy. I'm working twelve hours a day.

Wendy Twelve hours! You're going to kill yourself!

Charles Well, what can I do?

Wendy Perhaps you should change your job.

Charles I can't . . . I need the money!

Exercise

Write sentences with *should* and *shouldn't*:
1 Your friend wants to lose weight.
2 Someone wants to learn your language.
3 Your friend wants to be a millionaire . . . quickly!

39 An evening out

Steve Shall we go out tonight?
Carol O.K. Let's go to a restaurant.
Steve Which one?
Carol How about 'The Flamenco'?
Steve 'The Flamenco'? Which one's that?
Carol Don't you remember? That's the one that serves sea-food . . .
Steve Oh, yes!

Carol Look over there!
Steve Where?
Carol In the corner . . . It's Jack West, isn't it?
Steve Where? I can't see him . . .
Carol There! He's the one that's wearing a black suit.
Steve Oh! The one that's talking so loudly . . . what about him?
Carol He used to be at college with us. He was the only one that didn't pass the exams.
Steve Hmm, he looks very successful. What does he do now?
Carol Nothing. He doesn't have to work.
Steve Why not?
Carol Well, you remember, don't you? He married Patty Hetty.
Steve Patty Hetty?
Carol Yes, the girl that inherited a fortune. Her father was a millionaire.
Steve Ah, yes . . . isn't she the one that killed herself?
Carol That's right . . . and he got all the money!

That's the one that did it!

Look at this

A boy broke the window.
Is that the boy?
Yes, that's the boy that broke the window.

 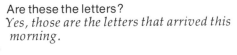

Some letters arrived this morning.
Are these the letters?
Yes, those are the letters that arrived this morning.

Now you do the same.

A man met the Queen.
Is that the man?

They won the medals.
Are those the men?

A car crashed.
Is that the car?

A dog attacked the postman.
Is that the dog?

40 I've been waiting...

Chris Hello, Miss Wright. Is the boss in?
Miss Wright Yes, Chris, he is. He's in his office . . . and he's waiting for you.
Chris Oh . . . what time did he arrive?
Miss Wright He arrived at twenty to ten.
Chris Twenty to ten! So he's been waiting for twenty minutes!

Diane Hello, Judy. You've been sitting here for an hour! Where's your husband?
Judy Oh, he's dancing with Mrs Winston.
Diane Oh, yes . . . he's dancing very well. Has he been dancing all evening?
Judy Yes, he has . . . but he hasn't been dancing with me!

Mrs Baker Hello, Mrs Parker . . . are you waiting to see Doctor Savage?
Mrs Parker Hello, Mrs Baker. Yes, I am.
Mrs Baker How long have you been waiting?
Mrs Parker I've been waiting since nine o'clock.
Mrs Baker Ah, so you haven't been waiting long. It's only ten past nine now.
Mrs Parker No, no, I haven't. I've been reading this magazine. It's very interesting. There's an article about operations.

Pam Eric! Call the waiter again!
Eric I've been trying to call him.
Pam Eric! We've been sitting here for twenty minutes . . . and I'm not going to wait any longer!
Eric I'm sorry, dear . . . but he's talking to that girl.
Pam Yes, he's been talking to her since we came in.
Eric Waiter!
Waiter Yes, sir . . . Do you want the bill?
Eric The bill! We haven't seen the menu yet.

Exercise

He's waiting. He arrived five minutes ago.
He's been waiting for five minutes.

They're waiting. They arrived at nine o'clock.
They've been waiting since nine o'clock.

Continue

1 She's sitting in the armchair. She sat down ten minutes ago.
2 They're watching television. They switched it on at eight o'clock.
3 He's writing a letter. He started fifteen minutes ago.
4 She's listening to the radio. She switched it on at seven thirty.
5 They're talking to each other. They met five minutes ago.

41 A court case

A few months ago, there was a bank robbery in Stanford. The police arrested a man and a woman. They're in court now. A woman saw the robbery. She's standing in the witness box. The judge and the twelve members of the jury are listening to her. A lawyer is asking her some questions.

Lawyer Now, Miss Dexter. You saw the bank robbery, didn't you?
Miss Dexter Yes, I did.
Lawyer You saw a man, didn't you?
Miss Dexter That's right. I saw him when he went into the bank and when he came out.
Lawyer Now, look around the court . . . can you see that man?
Miss Dexter Yes, he's the man I saw.
Lawyer He wasn't alone when he went into the bank, was he?
Miss Dexter No, he was with a woman.
Lawyer Now, look around the court again . . . can you see that woman?
Miss Dexter Yes, there! She's the woman I saw.
Lawyer I see, Miss Dexter. Now look at the man and woman again. This is very important. Are you absolutely sure about them?
Miss Dexter Absolutely sure. They're the people I saw.
Lawyer Now, Miss Dexter. What was the man wearing when he went into the bank?

Miss Dexter I don't remember everything . . . but I remember his hat and his bag.
Lawyer Look at the hat on the table. Is that the hat?
Miss Dexter Yes, that's the hat he was wearing.
Lawyer . . . and the bag?
Miss Dexter Yes, that's the bag he was carrying.
Lawyer Do you remember anything about the woman?
Miss Dexter Yes. She was wearing a blonde wig and black platform shoes.
Lawyer How do you know it was a wig, Miss Dexter?
Miss Dexter Because it fell off when she was running to the car.
Lawyer Look at the wig on the table. Is that the wig?
Miss Dexter Yes, that's the wig she was wearing.
Lawyer . . . and the shoes . . . look at the shoes.
Miss Dexter Yes, they're the shoes she was wearing.
Lawyer Thank you, Miss Dexter.

Exercise

They're the people.
She saw them.
They're the people she saw.

1 She's the girl.
   He kissed her.
2 Those are the shoes.
   He was wearing them.
3 That's the house.
   He's going to buy it.
4 That's the book.
   She's been reading it.

42 The Empty Chair

A friend of mine, Rob Jenkins, almost had a nervous breakdown last year. I told him to go to the doctor.

Doctor Hello, Mr Jenkins. What can I do for you?
Mr Jenkins Well, doctor . . . I'm very tense and nervous. I haven't been able to sleep for several days.
Doctor Hmm . . . have you been working hard?
Mr Jenkins Oh, yes. I've been very busy. I've been working twelve hours a day.
Doctor Have you been taking any pills?
Mr Jenkins No, but I've been smoking too much, and I've been drinking a lot of coffee.
Doctor Well, you should take a holiday. You should go somewhere quiet and peaceful, like Cornwall. Why don't you go there?

Rob decided to go to Cornwall the next weekend. Penquay was a very small fishing village on the north coast of Cornwall. There were no trains or buses to Penquay, so he had to drive. It was a long journey, and Rob arrived late on Friday evening. The landlady of the guest house, Mrs Doone, answered the door and showed him to his room. Rob was very tired and went straight to bed. He slept well and didn't wake up until nine o'clock the next morning.

Rob went downstairs for breakfast. Because there were no other guests, Mrs Doone invited him to have breakfast with her and her daughter, Catherine. Catherine was already sitting in the dining room. She was about thirteen years old, with long, black hair and clear, grey eyes. Mrs Doone went to the kitchen to prepare breakfast. Rob and Catherine looked at each other nervously for a few seconds.

Rob There are four places at the table. Is there another guest?
Catherine Oh, no . . . we never talk about the empty place.
Rob The empty place? What do you mean?
Catherine Well, that used to be my father's place.
Rob 'Used to be?' I don't understand.
Catherine My father was a fisherman. Three years ago he went out in his boat, and he never returned.
Rob What happened to him?
Catherine Nobody knows. They searched everywhere, but they found nothing. My mother always keeps that place for him, and she makes his breakfast every morning. She thinks he'll come back. That's a photograph of him . . . over there, on the wall. My mother's been waiting for him for three years.

Rob said nothing, but he looked very worried. At that moment Mrs Doone returned. She poured four cups of tea, and put one cup in the empty place. Rob looked more worried and he stared at the empty chair. Suddenly, he heard footsteps outside the door and a tall man, with a black beard, walked into the room. Rob looked terrified. It was the man in the photograph! He jumped up and ran out of the room.

Man Who was that? What's the matter?
Mrs Doone I don't know. I don't understand. He's a guest from London. He arrived last night while you were asleep.
Man Catherine! Do you know anything about this?
Catherine No, I don't, father. But he's here because he's very nervous. He says he's hiding here because a tall man with a black beard is trying to kill him.
Man Catherine, have you been telling stories again?
Catherine (*laughing*) Stories, father? Me?

43 How long? How much?

Bank Manager Come in. You're Mr Carson, aren't you? Please sit down.
Mr Carson Thank you.
Bank Manager What can I do for you, Mr Carson?
Mr Carson Well, I want to borrow some money.
Bank Manager What for?
Mr Carson I want to buy a car. I've been saving for two years.
Bank Manager Ah, how much have you saved?
Mr Carson I've saved about a thousand pounds.

Exercise 1

He/two years/£1000.
He's been saving for two years. He's saved £1000.

Now you do the same:
They/six months/£800.
She/a year/£1500.
We/three years/£3000.

Judith What are you reading?
Maureen *The Godfather*. It's about the Mafia in America. John told me to read it.
Judith It's a very long book.
Maureen I know. I've been reading it for a month, and I haven't finished it yet!
Judith How many pages have you read?
Maureen About 400. I don't like long books.
Judith Neither do I!

Exercise 2

I/*The Godfather*/a month/400 pages.
I've been reading The Godfather *for a month. I've read 400 pages.*

Now you do the same:
He/*War and Peace*/a week/250 pages.
She/*Moby Dick*/a fortnight/300 pages.
I/*Airport*/ten days/500 pages.

Attendant Petrol, sir?
Motorist Please . . . fill it up.
Attendant Which grade?
Motorist Four star. It's nearly empty. I've been driving all day.
Attendant Oh, how far have you driven?
Motorist About 400 miles. I've driven from Scotland.
Attendant Oh, that's a long way. Shall I check the oil and water?
Motorist Please.

Exercise 3

They/all day/400 miles/Scotland.
They've been driving all day. They've driven 400 miles. They've driven from Scotland.

Now you do the same:
He/since nine o'clock/300 miles/Yorkshire.
We/for six hours/250 miles/Cornwall.
She/since breakfast/200 miles/North Wales.

Karen Hello, Jenny. Are you still working? It's time for lunch.
Jenny I know. But I haven't finished these letters yet. They're important. Mr Power wants them this afternoon.
Karen How long have you been typing?
Jenny Since nine o'clock. I didn't stop for coffee.
Karen How many have you done?
Jenny Most of them. There are only two left.
Karen Well, do them after lunch.
Jenny No. I'll do them now.
Karen O.K. See you this afternoon.

44 Look!

Nick Owen is a guide for Britannia tours. Some new tourists have just arrived in Exmouth. He's showing them around the town.
'I'm sure you'll enjoy your stay here. There's the beach that's the safest for swimmers. The other beaches aren't as good. And that's the shop that sells picnic lunches. Over there's the shop that sells souvenirs. I'll meet you back here at four o'clock.'

Paul's showing Angela some holiday photos.
'Look . . . this is the hotel I stayed in . . . and here's the restaurant I used to go to. I used to eat there every day. This is the beach we used to lie on. It was a marvellous holiday.'

Anne's just had an accident. She's telling a policeman about it.
'The car in front of me stopped suddenly. I managed to stop, but the van behind me didn't. It hit my car, and pushed it into the car in front. There's my car. There's the van that hit my car. And that's the car my car hit.'

Paul's showing Angela an old school photo.
'The headmaster's in the middle. He's the one that taught us Latin. His lessons were very boring. The fat one on the left is Mr Bunter. He's the one that used to hit us with a cane. Mr Cherry's on the right. He's the one that taught us French . . . and football. I was never bored in his lessons!'

This is a picture of Ronald Rigg. He's the man the police arrested yesterday. He's standing next to P.C. Martin. Martin's the policeman that caught him.

Exercise

Look at these examples:
She's the girl. I love her.
She's the girl I love.

He's the man. He met me.
He's the man that met me.

That's the plane. I flew in it.
That's the plane I flew in.

It's the gun. It killed him.
It's the gun that killed him.

Now you do the same:
He's the man. He visited Buenos Aires.
She's the girl. I know her.
They're the shoes. I was wearing them.
That's the man. He lives near me.
There's the bridge. We crossed it.
There's the house. We used to live in it.
Those are the parcels. They arrived this morning.
That's the woman. She'll be Prime Minister one day.
He's the man. I spoke to him.
It's the car. It crashed.

45 Another letter from Mary

68 rue des Alpes,
Paris.
September 16th

Dear John,
   I got your letter this morning. I'm very pleased that you'll be able to come to Paris next month. Don't worry about hotels. There's the Hôtel Napoléon just around the corner. That's the hotel I used to stay at before I found my flat. I'm sure you won't be bored here. Paris is a very exciting city. I go to school in the mornings only, so we'll be able to see each other every afternoon.
   I've bought a second-hand cassette-player. It isn't as good as a language laboratory, but I've been listening to myself at home and I've been able to improve my pronunciation. Mr. Oliver — he's the teacher who's been teaching me since I arrived — says I should stay here longer. I'm not sure that it's a good idea. What do you think? I still like Paris and I'm happy here, but I'm not satisfied with my French yet. I miss my family ... and, of course, I miss you. Write back to me soon.
    All my love,
     Mary.

Look at this example

I/postcard/afternoon.
I/happy/you/able/here/week.
I got your postcard this afternoon. I'm happy that you'll be able to come here next week.

Now use these words, and write a letter.

I/postcard/afternoon.
I/happy/you/able/here/week.
Not worry/accommodation.
There/Hotel Romantica/corner.
That/hotel/I/stay/before/landlady.
I/sure/you/bored.
This/interesting town.
I/college/afternoons/so/we/meet/evening.

I/new tape-recorder.
Tape-recorder/portable/cassette-player.
I/myself/home, and I/improve/accent.
Mr Smith ... he/teacher/me/came here ... says I/longer.
I think/good idea.
What/think?
I/this town and/happy/but I/not satisfied/English yet.
I/everybody. Write/soon.

46 Booking in advance

A Hello. Old England Restaurant. Can I help you?
B Yes. I'd like to book a table for tonight.
A Yes, sir. What time?
B Eight o'clock.
A Certainly, sir. For how many people?
B There are ten of us.
A Ten of you! We don't usually accept large parties, sir.
B I know, but we are regular customers.
A What's your name please, sir?
B Richard Burton.
A Mr Burton . . . of course that'll be all right. We'll put two tables together.

tonight/
8 pm/ten
tomorrow night/
9.30/eight
Saturday evening/
8.45/seven
next Friday/
10 pm/nine

C I'd like two seats for the concert on Thursday evening.
D Yes. Where would you like to sit?
C I'm not sure.
D Well, here's a seating plan of the concert hall.
C How much is it in the middle?
D £6.
C £6! That's a little too expensive for us. How much is it there . . . at the back?
D £2.
C That's fine. What time does the concert start?
D At half past seven, sir.

concert/
Thursday evening/
7.30
pop concert/
Friday night/
8.00
ballet/
Saturday afternoon/
3.00
opera
Monday evening/
8.30
at the front – £7
in the middle – £6
on the left – £5
on the right – £5

E Have you got any seats left for the Stratford excursion?
F Yes, sir. There are a few seats left.
E Is that the one that goes to Oxford as well?
F That's right.
E How long does the whole excursion take?
F Approximately ten hours, sir.
E Shall I pay you now?
F If you don't mind, sir.

Excursions
Stratford and Oxford
 (10 hours)
Cambridge and Ely
 (12 hours)
Bath and Bristol
 (7 hours)
Winchester and Poole
 (9 hours)

G Good morning. Unisex Hairdressers.
H Good morning. I'd like to make an appointment, please, for three o'clock this afternoon. With Marcel.
G Let me see. I'm afraid Marcel's busy at three, madam.
H Oh dear. Marcel always does my hair.
G I'm sorry, madam.
H Well, how about four o'clock?
G I'm terribly sorry, madam. Marcel's busy all afternoon.
H What a nuisance!
G I'm very, very sorry, madam. But you should always book well in advance.

3 pm/Marcel
2.40/Paolo
12.30/Pierre
5.00/Jeremy

47 A new job

Patti Alice! Have you seen this ad in the paper?

Alice Oh, yes . . . but I'm not interested in finding a new job. I've been here since I left school. I like working here.

Patti Really? I've only been here for two months and I'm already tired of doing the same thing every day. I want some adventure!

Alice Adventure! There's too much 'adventure' in New York. People are afraid of walking in the streets.

Patti Oh, come on! It's not that bad . . . and the salaries are fantastic!

Alice I'm not interested in earning more money. I've got enough now.

Patti Ah, yes . . . but you live at home with your parents.

Alice But I like living with my parents. What's wrong with that?

Patti Nothing. But I like being independent. I like travelling, I enjoy meeting new people. I'm going to apply for the job.

Alice Well, good luck!

Exercise 1

Answer these questions:

What do you like doing in	spring?
	summer?
	autumn?
	winter?

| What do you like doing | at weekends? |
| | on holiday? |

Exercise 2

I don't like watching television.
Write five true sentences.

Exercise 3

flying
He's afraid of flying.

Write sentences using:
going to the dentist
losing his job
dying

Exercise 4

I'm interested in learning English.
I'm not interested in studying history.
Write true sentences.

48 The weather forecast

Paul and Judy live in Birmingham. It's a large city in the Midlands. They're planning a weekend holiday.

Paul I know, Judy! Why don't we go to Scotland?
Judy It's a very long way.
Paul Oh, it isn't too far. Anyway, the motorway's very good, so we can get there quickly.
Judy But Scotland's often cold at this time of the year. It may snow!
Paul Well, yes . . . it may . . . but I don't think it will.
Judy I'm not sure. It is February, and I'm frightened of driving in snow. And we may not be able to find a hotel. They may be closed.
Paul Oh, that's no problem. I can book a hotel by phone.
Judy Well, perhaps it's not a bad idea. We may have beautiful weather.
Paul Oh, we'll enjoy ourselves anyway. Let's watch the weather forecast on television. We may not go to Scotland, we may go to Wales or London. We can decide after the forecast . . . .

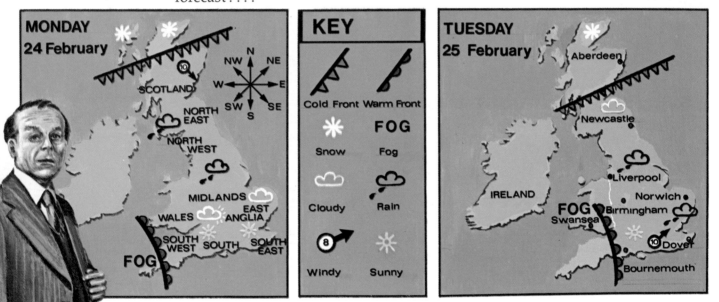

Good evening, and here is the weather forecast for tomorrow. Northern Scotland will be cold, and there may be snow over high ground. In the north of England it will be a wet day and rain may move into Wales and the Midlands during the afternoon. East Anglia will be generally dry, but it will be dull and cloudy. In southern England it will be a bright clear day with sunshine, but it may rain during the evening. In the south west it may be foggy during the morning, but the afternoon will be clear. It may be windy later in the day.

Exercise 1

Where's Aberdeen? It's in the north of Scotland.

Write questions and answers for:
Newcastle, Liverpool, Swansea, Birmingham, Norwich, Dover, and Bournemouth.

Exercise 2

What will the weather be like in Bournemouth? It will be warm and sunny.
What will the weather be like in Norwich? It may rain.

Write questions and answers for all the towns.

Exercise 3

What will the weather be like here tomorrow?

49 A restaurant kitchen

Waitress Hurry up, Chef! The customers have been waiting for ten minutes. They're hungry and they're getting angry!

Chef I know, I know . . . but I've only got one pair of hands! You'll have to help me.

Waitress Help you? That's not my job . . . I'm a waitress, not a cook.

Chef Well, both of my assistants are off work.

Waitress Oh, all right. What shall I do first?

Chef Well, start putting the meat on the plates and I'll prepare the vegetables.

Waitress O.K. Is that enough meat?

Chef Hmm . . . that's a bit too much . . . take a bit off.

Waitress What about potatoes?

Chef Oh, put on plenty of potatoes . . . they're cheap . . . and lots of peas.

Waitress All right, all right. Can I take them now?

Chef Have you put the sauce on yet?

Waitress Eh? Oh no, I haven't. Where is it?

Chef Here it is.

Waitress Oh, there isn't quite enough sauce here.

Chef There's plenty in that pan over there.

Waitress Ah, yes . . . I've got it.

Chef Fine, now you can begin taking the plates to the customers.

Waitress Ow! They're hot!

Chef Well, use a cloth . . . and don't carry too many plates. You may drop them.

Waitress Oh, I won't drop them. I've never dropped a plate in my life!

Exercise

Thirty-two people have bought tickets for an excursion.
This is a forty-seater bus. *There are plenty of seats.*
This is a thirty-seater bus. *There aren't quite enough seats.*

1

Eight people are coming to dinner.
We've got twelve wine glasses.
We've got only seven chairs.

2

This car costs £3000. Both Hazel and Barry want to buy it.
Hazel's got £4000.
Barry's got only £2900.

50 Asking for directions

A Excuse me!
B Yes?
A I'm looking for the Men's Clothes department.
B Ah, yes, sir. It's on the fourth floor. The lift's over there.
A Thank you . . . but I'll use the stairs. I need the exercise!

Harridges
- 5th floor
  Cafeteria Toilets
- 4th floor
  Men's Clothes
- 3rd floor
  Ladies' Clothes
- 2nd floor
  Furniture
- 1st floor
  Household Goods
- Ground floor
  Cosmetics
- Basement
  Food Hall

C Good morning. Can I help you?
D Yes, I've got an appointment with Mrs Truman, the Sales Manager.
C What time is your appointment, sir?
D Half past eleven.
C Right. Go up those stairs to the first floor. Take the corridor on the left. Mrs Truman's office is the third door on the right. You can't miss it.
D Thank you.
C Oh, sir . . .
D Yes?
C Don't bother to knock. Go straight in. She's expecting you.

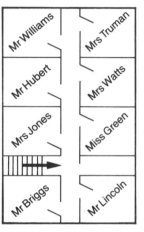

Mr Williams / Mrs Truman
Mr Hubert / Mrs Watts
Mrs Jones / Miss Green
Mr Briggs / Mr Lincoln

E Excuse me!
F Yes?
E I'm lost! Is this the way to Brighton?
F No, I'm afraid it isn't. You're going the wrong way. This is the Portsmouth Road.
E Oh, dear. Can you tell me the way to Brighton?
F Yes, turn round and go back to the roundabout. Take the third exit . . . that's the A272.
E The A272?
F That's right. You'll see signposts to Brighton from there.

London A3
Brighton A272
A272 Southampton
Portsmouth A3

G Fares, please . . .
H Two to Market Street, please.
G 36p.
H Can you tell me when we get there?
G O.K.
H Thanks a lot.

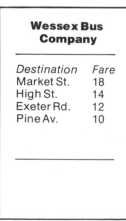

Wessex Bus Company

Destination	Fare
Market St.	18
High St.	14
Exeter Rd.	12
Pine Av.	10

51 Air-sea rescue

This is the Radio 1 Newsdesk. In Dorset, a helicopter is trying to rescue a man who has fallen down a cliff. He's lying on a small beach. An air-sea rescue helicopter has arrived at the scene, and one of the crew has climbed down a ladder to the beach. He's speaking to a doctor by radio.

Crewman Hello. Can you hear me, doctor?

Doctor Yes, I can hear you clearly. Is he unconscious?

Crewmen No, he's conscious. But he looks pretty bad.

Doctor O.K. Ask him if he can move.

Crewman Can you move?

Man No . . .

Doctor Ask him if he's in pain.

Crewman Are you in pain?

Man Oh . . . yes . . .

Doctor Ask him where it hurts.

Crewman Where does it hurt?

Man It's my back.

Doctor Right. Don't move him. I'm coming down.

Frank Aitken is the editor of *The Daily News*. He's sending a trainee journalist to interview the American singer, Bob Sonata.

'Now, I've arranged the interview for four o'clock . . . at his hotel. Ask him lots of questions. You know . . . ask him if he likes England. Ask him what his next record will be, when he recorded it . . . and ask him where. Ask him all the usual questions . . . but don't . . . don't ask him how old he is. O.K.?'

Practice

Now you are the editor. You're sending a journalist to interview these famous people. Tell him or her what questions to ask.

The Queen of England/a film star/
Paul McCartney/a famous footballer

Exercise 1

Ask him if he's married.
Are you married?

1 Ask him if he's a student.
2 Ask him if he's got a car.
3 Ask him if he can swim.
4 Ask him if he likes tea.
5 Ask him if he enjoys learning English.
6 Ask him if he got up early this morning.
7 Ask him if he's been to Brazil.

Exercise 2

Is she bored?
I don't know. You ask her if she's bored.

1 Has she got any brothers?
2 Can she drive?
3 Does she speak French?
4 Does she like watching television?
5 Did she go out last night?
6 Has she ever met the Queen?
7 Will she be at school tomorrow?

Exercise 3

Ask him where he lives.
Where do you live?

1 Ask him what his job is.
2 Ask him who he met yesterday.
3 Ask him when he arrived at school.
4 Ask him why he's laughing.
5 Ask him how he goes to work.
6 Ask him how far it is to London.
7 Ask him how much money he's got.

Exercise 4

Where did he buy his watch?
I don't know. You ask him where he bought his watch.

1 Who did he speak to last night?
2 When did they get married?
3 What has she done today?
4 How many children have they got?
5 Why must he go to the police station?
6 How old is she?
7 How much did she pay for her car?

52 UFO

Ronald and Jean were driving along a quiet country road in southern England. They were on the way to Westbury. It was nearly midnight.

Jean Ron . . . look over there. There's something in the sky. What is it?

Ron I don't know what it is. It's probably a plane.

Jean I don't think so. It's too big . . . and too bright.

Ron Oh, no.

Jean What's the matter?

Ron The engine's stopped.

Jean Why has it stopped?

Ron I don't know why it's stopped. We'll have to find a garage.

Jean Is there one near here?

Ron Yes, there's one in the next village . . . but I don't know if it's open. It's very late.

Suddenly there was a loud noise, and a big, bright silver object flew low over their car. It stopped in mid-air, turned round and flew back over their car. Then it went straight up into the sky and disappeared.

Jean Oh, Ron! What was that?

Ron Eh? Don't ask me . . . I've got no idea what it was!

Jean Oh, I'm frightened . . . let's go.

Ron We can't . . . the engine isn't working.

Jean Oh . . . try it again!

Ron That's strange. It's O.K. now. I wonder why it wasn't working?

Jean Oh, Ron . . . do you think it was a UFO?

Ron I don't know . . . I really don't. We should phone the police.

Jean Ron . . . do you think they'll believe us?

Exercise 1

Where did it come from? (They don't know.)
They don't know where it came from.

1 What was it? (He's got no idea.)
2 Why wasn't it working? (They wonder.)
3 Where did it go? (She doesn't know.)
4 What will the police say? (They've got no idea.)

Exercise 2

Was it a UFO? (He's got no idea.)
He's got no idea if it was a UFO.

1 Did it come from another planet? (They wonder.)
2 Is the garage open? (He doesn't know.)
3 Was it a dream? (We don't know.)
4 Will the police believe them? (They've got no idea.)

DAILY NEWS

EVENING EDITION

9p

THURSDAY, JANUARY 12th

No. 732 142

SUPERTANKER DISASTER

Danger to holiday beaches

Holiday towns and fishing villages in the South-West are preparing to fight the oil pollution which is threatening local beaches.

Yesterday there was a collision in the English Channel between the "S.P. Titan", which is one of the biggest oil tankers in the world, and a Dutch cargo ship. The collision happened in thick fog late last night, and damaged the tanker's engines. It drifted onto rocks, and broke in half. The tanker was carrying 100,000 tons of crude oil, and an oil slick is moving slowly towards Cornwall. Helicopters rescued both crews, and nobody died in the collision. Hundreds of small boats, which are carrying detergents, are spraying the oil.

CORNWALL

OIL SLICK
✕

WEATHER

There may be snow in parts of Scotland. In Northern England there probably won't be snow, but there may be heavy showers. Showery weather will also reach the Midlands later. It will be a cloudy day in the South, with some thunder and lightning in the south-east.

Temperatures: average for the time of year. Winds: light to moderate. Strong in Scotland.

WHERE'S MY HOUSE?

Mr Jeff Shepherd, who lives in Watermouth, returned home from work last night and couldn't find his house. It was on the edge of a cliff, and during the afternoon it fell into the sea. There may be more cliff falls, and local residents are spending the night in a school. The police have warned people not to return to their homes.

Surprise for a thief

Somewhere in London, a thief is going to get a nasty surprise today. Last night someone stole a van in Baker Street. The van belonged to London Zoo, and in the back were two large boxes. They contained poisonous snakes. The van was on its way from London Airport to the Zoo. The thief took the van from outside a shop while the driver was buying cigarettes!

WORDPLAY

A	I	O
L	E	M
N	P	C

How many words can you make? Every word must contain the letter "E", and use some of the other letters in the box.

You can only use each letter once. It's possible to make one 9-letter word.

30 words or more *Excellent.* 20 words or more *Very good.* 15 words or more *Good.*

54 A mugging

1

One night, Mrs Riley, an elderly widow, was walking along a dark, London street. She was carrying her handbag in one hand and a plastic carrier bag in the other. There was nobody else in the street except two youths. They were standing in a dark shop doorway. One of them was very tall with fair hair, the other was short and fat with a beard and moustache.

2

The youths waited for a few moments, and then ran quickly and quietly towards Mrs Riley. The tall youth held her from behind while the other youth tried to snatch her handbag.

3

Suddenly, Mrs Riley threw the tall youth over her shoulder. He crashed into the other youth and they both landed on the ground. Without speaking, Mrs Riley struck both of them on the head with her handbag, and walked calmly away.

4

The two surprised youths were still sitting on the ground when Mrs Riley crossed the street towards a door with a lighted sign above it. Mrs Riley paused, turned round, smiled at the youths and walked into the South West London Judo Club.

Exercise

Write the story below. The words will help you.

5

Last night Mr Lester/ middle-aged widower/ Birmingham street. He/briefcase/umbrella. There/nobody else/ two men. They/side-street. One/big/black, curly hair. The other/thin/ bald head.

6

They/few seconds/and/ walk/slowly/silently/ Mr Lester. The big man/hold/ behind. The thin one/try/ steal/ Mr Lester/briefcase.

7

Suddenly Mr Lester/ big one/shoulder. He/collide with/ thin one. They/land/pavement. Mr Lester/strike/ umbrella/and/walk/ quickly away.

8

The two astonished men/sit/ground. Mr Lester/cross/ road/towards/door/ painted sign. Mr Lester/stop/ turn/laugh/walk into/Central Birmingham Karate Club.

55 An important visitor

The platform of Portsbridge station is full of people. They're waiting for an important visitor – the Queen. They're expecting her to arrive soon. She's going to open a new secondary school – Portsbridge Comprehensive. The Mayor's secretary is telling him about the plans for the day.

She'll be here soon. We'll wait until we see the train.

1 When the train stops, the band will start playing.
2 Your son will give her some flowers when she gets off the train.
3 You'll make a speech before she leaves the station.
4 As soon as she arrives at the school, the children will begin cheering.
5 After she opens the school, we'll go to the Town Hall.
6 When she gets to the Town Hall, you'll make another speech.
7 After you make the speech, we'll have lunch.
8 Before she leaves Portsbridge, you'll give her a present from the town.

Exercise 1

When/see him/say 'Hello'.
When I see him, I'll say 'Hello'.

1 When/see a garage/buy some petrol.
2 After/have breakfast/clean my teeth.
3 As soon as/wake up/get up.
4 Before/go to bed/switch off the light.

Exercise 2

Write long answers:
What'll happen when the train stops?
Who'll make a speech before she leaves the station?
When will the children begin cheering?
What'll they do after she opens the school?

Exercise 3

Write answers:
What'll you do when you get home tonight?
What'll you do after you have dinner?
What'll you do before you go to bed?
What'll you do as soon as you get up?

56 General Hospital

Maternity Ward

Mr Wallace is in the maternity ward. His wife's going to have a baby.

Nurse Hello . . . you're Mr Wallace, aren't you? Have you been waiting long?

Mr Wallace Not really. Is there any news?

Nurse Not yet. We'll tell you as soon as there is. Have you thought of any names for the baby?

Mr Wallace Oh yes! If it's a girl, we'll call her Victoria, and if it's a boy we'll call him Jason.

Operating Theatre

David Foster has had a serious accident. His wife's outside the operating theatre now.

Doctor Mrs Foster? I'm Dr. Payne.

Mrs Foster Oh, Doctor! How is he?

Doctor Well, I'm afraid we'll have to operate.

Mrs Foster Oh, no! He's always been afraid of operations.

Doctor Don't worry. If we operate now, he'll be all right.

Mrs Foster Oh, Doctor. Do you really have to?

Doctor I'm afraid so. He's lost a lot of blood. If we don't operate, he'll die!

Ward Ten

Mr Frampton has just arrived at the hospital. He's going to have a minor operation tomorrow.

Sister This is your bed, Mr Frampton.

Mr Frampton Oh, thank you, Sister.

Sister Now, could you get undressed and get into bed. There's a buzzer on the bedside table. If you press the button, someone will come at once.

Mr Frampton Oh, I'm sure I won't need anything . . .

Sister Well, don't forget . . . if you need anything, just press the button!

Casualty Department

Doctor Oh, dear! How did this happen?

Mother He was just playing with the saucepan, and he put it on his head . . . and now it's stuck!

Doctor Have you tried to get it off?

Mother No, I'm afraid of hurting him.

Doctor Yes, if we pull too hard, we'll hurt him.

Mother What are you going to do?

Doctor Well, if I don't get it off, he won't be able to eat!

Mother Oh, no!

Doctor I'm only joking. If I put some soap on his head, it'll come off easily.

Exercise

We/operate/he/be all right.
If we operate, he'll be all right.

Write sentences using:
You/take these pills/feel better.
You/eat too much/be ill.
He/press the button/nurse/come.
You/not take the medicine/not feel better.
You/no eat/not get well.
She/have a boy/call/Peter.

HAMPSHIRE GOLD CUP

KEY TO FORM

2 F 3 L 0 1
This list shows the
results of the horse's
six previous races.

1 First
2 Second
3 Third
4 Fourth
0 Unplaced
L Last
F Fell

KEY TO ODDS

3 – 1
If you bet one pound,
and the horse wins, you'll
get three pounds.

KEY TO NATIONALITY

GB Britain
IRL Ireland
F France
D Germany
NL Holland
USA United States
NZ New Zealand

HAMPSHIRE GOLD CUP

Two miles. Prize money £50,000

number	name		odds	form					
1	Black Beauty	(GB)	20–1	0	0	4	0	0	3
2	Irish Prince	(IRL)	3–1	3	4	3	3	1	0
3	Concorde	(F)	4–1	1	F	0	0	2	3
4	White Rum	(GB)	1–1 evens	1	1	1	1	1	1
5	Kentucky Moon	(USA)	14–1	2	0	0	0	4	3
6	Cash Register	(NZ)	2–1	3	2	2	3	0	1
7	Ferdinand III	(D)	33–1	0	0	0	0	0	0
8	Chestnut Mare	(IRL)	25–1	0	0	4	0	0	0
9	Dobbin	(GB)	100–1	L	L	L	F	L	L
10	Sylvester Stallion	(F)	10–1	4	4	2	F	0	1
11	Tricky Dicky	(USA)	66–1	0	F	0	F	L	F
12	Trigger	(NL)	50–1	0	L	0	0	0	4

Horse-racing is a very popular sport in Britain. There are over 11,000 horses in training, and there is a race meeting almost every day of the year. Some of the prizes are worth thousands of pounds and some of the horses are worth millions. Horses from all over the world enter for the big races. People bet on the horses, and if they are lucky, they can win a lot of money. Some people spend a lot of time studying the form of the horses, others just guess! Look at the list of horses for the Hampshire Gold Cup. Study it, and try to choose the winner.

Ask each other these questions

Which horse have you chosen?
What number is it?
Where does it come from?
What are the odds?
Why did you choose it?
Has it won before?
Has it been second/third/fourth/last?
Has it fallen?
How much are you going to bet?
If your horse wins, how much will you get?

'It's a lovely day here at Hurstwood Park. The horses are ready for today's big race – the Hampshire Gold Cup. And they're off! They've all started well. They're racing towards the first bend, and Dobbin's in the lead! Concorde's second and Chestnut Mare's third. Now they're approaching the first fence. And Dobbin's fallen . . . but the jockey looks all right . . . and now Concorde's in front. White Rum, the favourite, is at the back. Now they're entering the second bend . . . and they're all over the second fence . . . Cash Register has just passed Concorde, and Sylvester Stallion has moved into third place . . . then Irish Prince, then Tricky Dicky . . . now they're coming round the third bend . . . and it's a very close race . . . and they've all jumped the third fence . . . and the favourite, White Rum, is coming through . . . the crowd is cheering wildly . . . they're over the last fence . . . there's only 300 metres to go . . . and all the horses are in a line . . . I can't see which one's in front . . . it's very, very close . . . it's a photo finish! What a race! But we'll have to wait for the result . . . .'

58 On the road

Ann Ben! You can't park here! There's a double yellow line.

Ben Oh, we'll be back in a few minutes. It's O.K.

Ann Oh, no, it isn't. You'll get a parking ticket if you leave it here.

Ben No, I won't. It's half past five. All the traffic wardens have gone home.

Ann Ben!

Ben Yes?

Warden Is this your car, sir?

a double yellow line
a bus stop
a pedestrian crossing
a 'no parking' sign'

P.C. Excuse me. May I see your licence?

Ben I'm afraid I've left it at home.

P.C. In that case you'll have to take it to the police station within five days.

Ben But . . . but why?

P.C. You were speeding, sir.

Ben But I was only doing 35!

P.C. There's a 30 miles an hour speed limit on this road, sir.

Ben Is there? I didn't see the sign . . .

P.C. Well, sir. We've been following you.

Ben So you were doing 35, too.

P.C. No, sir. We were doing 60 miles an hour . . . and we couldn't catch you!

35 mph/30 mph speed limit
45 mph/40 mph speed limit
55 mph/50 mph speed limit
75 mph/70 mph speed limit

Man Hello . . . Wadley's Garage.

Ben Oh, good evening. I don't know if you can help me. My car's broken down.

Man We have a 24-hour breakdown service. Where are you?

Ben I'm on the A357 . . . just north of Ringbourne. My car's just past the Red Lion pub . . . it's a white M.G.

Man Do you know what's wrong with it?

Ben I've got no idea . . . but it won't start.

Man I'll send a mechanic out to you. He'll be there in about ten minutes.

A357/north
B342/south
A31/east
M3/west

Mechanic It's nothing serious, sir. You've run out of petrol.

Ben Oh! Can you tow me to the garage?

Mechanic That's not necessary. I've got a spare can of petrol in my truck.

Ben Shall I pay you now, or shall I come to the garage?

Mechanic You can pay me now.

Ben Will you take a cheque? I've run out of cash, too.

Mechanic Yes, that's O.K.

Ben Hold on . . . I can't find my cheque book!

You've run out of petrol/ a spare can of petrol

You haven't got enough oil/ some tins of oil

The radiator's empty/ some water

The battery's flat/ a new battery

59 A trip to Paris

13 Nelson Road
Moss Side
Manchester
M17 3JQ
1st October 1978

Dear Sir,

I would like to reserve a single room with private bathroom, for 3 nights from Friday, 15th October, to Sunday, 17th October, inclusive. Please let me know if you require a deposit. Could you confirm my reservation by return of post?

Yours faithfully
John Carter

Hôtel Napoléon

13, rue Pigalle, Montmartre, Paris. Telephone 126 63 238. Telex 28443 Honap, Paris.

PD/JL/3.10   3rd October, 1978

John Carter, Esq.,
13, Nelson Road,
Moss Side,
MANCHESTER,
England.

Dear Mr. Carter,

    Thank you for your letter of 1st October. We confirm your reservation for the nights of 15 - 17th October inclusive. It is not necessary to send a deposit. We look forward to seeing you, and hope that you will enjoy your stay with us.

                        Yours sincerely,

                        Pierre Douton.

                        Assistant Manager

Exercise 1

Now, write a letter to reserve a room at the Hotel Wellington, Waterloo Street, London.

Exercise 2

Now, write a reply from the hotel. Begin *Dear Mr . . . , Mrs . . . , Miss . . . ,* or *Ms . . .*

Exercise 3

Now, write a telegram to a friend. Tell him when you'll arrive home. You can use only twelve words.

Post Office International Telegram

This telegram will be charged at ordinary rate unless an indicator (URGENT, ELT, LT, or GLT) is inserted between the double hyphens before the address.

= URGENT =   BLOCK LETTERS THROUGHOUT PLEASE

TO MARY COLEMAN /68, RUE DES ALPES / PARIS
ARRIVING 19.45 FLIGHT BE 904 LOVE JOHN

Name and Address of Sender (Not to be Telegraphed)
JOHN CARTER / 13 NELSON RD / MOSS SIDE /
MANCHESTER / M17 3JQ   Telephone No. 061-123-4567

60 Emergency . . . 999

Operator Emergency. Which service, please?
Caller Police.
Police Police, here.
Caller I've just seen two cars crash into a security van. I think it's a robbery.
Police Where?
Caller Just outside the factory gates.
Police Which factory, sir?
Caller Croxley Engineering . . . in Brook Lane . . .

The first police car got to the factory three minutes later, but it was too late! The robbers had gone. They had knocked out one of the security guards and shot the other. They were both lying on the ground near the van. The thieves had taken all wages for the factory. The police called an ambulance, and questioned three people who had seen the robbery.

Operator Emergency. Which service, please?
Caller Fire.
Fire Fire Service.
Caller Come quickly! Fenley's Garage is on fire . . . the one in Churchill Road.
Fire We'll be there in two minutes . . .

The fire engine got to the garage just in time. The showroom was burning. Fortunately the fire hadn't reached the petrol pumps, and hadn't spread to neighbouring houses. The firemen were able to put it out quickly. The fire had started in the office. Someone had thrown a lighted cigarette into a waste-paper basket.

Operator Emergency. Which service, please?
Caller Ambulance . . .
Ambulance Ambulance service.
Caller Hurry . . . there's a boy . . . he's in the canal, and I don't think he can swim!
Ambulance Where are you, madam?
Caller Oh, sorry . . . near the bridge . . . the one in Balaclava Street.
Ambulance We're on our way!

When the ambulance arrived the boy was lying on the quay. A policeman had seen the boy in the water and had dived in and rescued him. The boy was all right. The policeman had given him artificial respiration. The ambulance took the boy and the policeman to hospital.

Exercise

3.00: The police arrived. 2.55: The robbers went.
When the police arrived, the robbers had gone.

7.00: He got to the airport. 6.50: The plane took off.
· · · ·
9.05: The student came into class. 9.00: The lesson started.
· · · ·
4.50: The helicopter arrived. 4.15: The boat sank.
· · · ·
11.20: She went out. 11.18: The rain stopped.
· · · ·

Readers' Letters

Have you ever had an embarrassing experience?
Last week we asked readers to tell us about embarrassing
experiences. We received hundreds of letters! Here is a
selection.

A smart teacher!

. . . My most embarrassing experience happened when I had just left university. I had just started teaching in a Liverpool secondary school. One morning my alarm clock didn't ring . . . I had forgotten to wind it up. I woke up at half past eight and school began at nine. I quickly washed, shaved, dressed, jumped into my car and drove to school. When I arrived the students had already gone into class. I didn't go to the staff room, but went straight into class. After two or three minutes the students began laughing, and I couldn't understand why! Suddenly I looked down and understood. I had put on one black shoe and one brown shoe!

Stanley Hooper, B.A., Preston, Lancs.

Hand in hand

The most embarrassing experience I've ever had, happened two years ago. My wife and I had driven into town to do some shopping. The streets were very busy and we were holding hands. Suddenly my wife saw a dress that she liked in a shop window, and stopped. I started looking at some radios in the next window. After a minute or two I reached for my wife's hand. There was a loud scream, and a woman slapped my face. I hadn't taken my wife's hand, I'd taken the hand of a complete stranger!

Len Bailey, Sheffield, Yorks.

A parking problem

My husband and I had decided to buy a new house, and I'd made an appointment to see our bank manager. I'd never met him before and I was a bit nervous. I drove into town and I was lucky enough to find a parking space outside the bank. I'd just started reversing into the space when another car drove into it. I was furious! I opened my window and shouted at the other driver. He ignored me and walked away. It took me twenty minutes to find another space. As soon as I had parked the car, I rushed back to the bank. I was ten minutes late for my interview. I went to the manager's office, knocked and walked in. The manager was sitting behind his desk. He was the man who had taken my parking space!

Kate Kirby, Portsmouth, Hants.

Why don't you write and tell us about your most embarrassing experience?

62 A ghost story

Edgar and Catherine are staying in a cottage in the New Forest. It belongs to Edgar's uncle, and they've borrowed it for the weekend. It's Friday night. They arrived an hour or two ago, and they're sitting in front of a log fire.

Catherine Oh, Edgar, this house is fantastic! I love old houses.

Edgar There's a ghost here, you know.

Catherine Edgar! Don't be silly . . . you're trying to frighten me

Edgar Not at all. I've been coming here for years. We used to stay here when I was a child. I saw the ghost myself once.

Catherine Edgar . . . this isn't funny. It's late at night. Anyway, I don't believe in ghosts.

Edgar Don't you? I do.

Catherine Where did you see the ghost?

Edgar Upstairs . . . in the bedroom.

Catherine Ha, ha. Did it have a white sheet over its head?

Edgar No, no. It was quite an ordinary ghost, really. He was wearing Victorian clothes.

Catherine He? Who?

Edgar The ghost, of course. I'll tell you about it. I'd been walking in the forest all day and I was really tired, so I went to bed early.

Catherine Had you had anything to drink?

Edgar No, no . . .

Catherine Well, go on . . . what happened?

Edgar I'd been in bed for two or three hours . . .

Catherine How do you know that it was a few hours?

Edgar There's an old grandfather clock in the bedroom. You'll see it when we go upstairs. Anyway, the man was standing beside it.

Catherine What man?

Edgar The ghost, of course.

Catherine What did you do?

Edgar Nothing.

Catherine What did he say?

Edgar Nothing . . . he just stared at me.

Catherine How did he get into the room? Had you locked the door?

Edgar Yes, I had . . . and the window. It was a cold, foggy night.

Catherine Was there a fireplace?

Edgar Yes, but it was too small for a man to get down. Anyway, there'd been a fire.

Catherine What did you do?

Edgar I sat up, and stared back at him. I was too shocked to move.

Catherine What happened? What happened?

Edgar Well, I don't know how long we'd been staring at each other, when suddenly I panicked and shouted . . . and he disappeared!

Catherine I don't believe it!

Edgar I didn't believe it myself at the time but when I told some people in the village, they believed me. Some of them had seen the ghost themselves. They could even describe him! If you ask them, they'll tell you.

Catherine Edgar . . . put some more wood on the fire. I'm going to sleep downstairs tonight!

Exercise

Do you believe in ghosts? Have you ever seen one?
Can you tell a ghost story?

63 Buying a present

In a record shop

Liz Have you got *Disco King*, please?

Assistant Who's it by?

Liz Soul Sensation. It's their latest single. It's just entered the charts . . . it's number nine this week!

Assistant Hold on . . . I'll just look . . . here you are.

Liz Oh, thanks . . . and have you got the new L.P. by the Rats.

Assistant What? *Teenage Revolution?* Oh, yes . . . we've got that . . . it's a fantastic album . . : you'll love it.

Liz Oh, it's not for me. It's for my grandmother. It's a birthday present!

		LAST/THIS WEEK'S TOP TEN
2	1	Love Me, Baby *Lorna Winter*
3	2	Teenage Revolution *The Rats*
1	3	You're my lady *Phil Crockett*
10	4	The Golden City *Fantasy*
4	5	Happy Summer Days *Danny Kleen*
5	6	Spaceship *Computer*
9	7	Midnight Blues *Mervyn Thomas*
6	8	Jamaica Rhythm *The Brothers*
7	9	Disco King *Soul Sensation*
8	10	The Breakthrough *Streamline Express*

In a jeweller's shop

Nigel I'm trying to find a Christmas present for my wife.

Assistant Yes, sir. What exactly are you looking for?

Nigel I'm not sure, really. Perhaps you can help me.

Assistant Right . . . I'll show you some bracelets.

Nigel No, I bought a bracelet for our wedding anniversary.

Assistant Maybe a ring, then. These rings are made of gold.

Nigel Yes . . . I like that one. What's the stone?

Assistant It's a diamond, sir . . . and it's only £2000!

Nigel Ah . . . well, perhaps you could show me some ear-rings, then.

bracelet
pendant
chain
ring
necklace
ear-rings

gold (Au)
silver (Ag)
platinum (Pt)
copper (Cu)

diamond
ruby
emerald
sapphire

In a toy shop

Mrs Cox Good morning. Perhaps you can advise me . . .

Assistant Yes, madam.

Mrs Cox I'm looking for a toy . . . for my nephew.

Assistant Oh, yes . . . how old is he?

Mrs Cox He'll be nine years old on Saturday.

Assistant Skateboards are still very popular.

Mrs Cox Hmm, I don't want him to hurt himself.

Assistant What about a drum set?

Mrs Cox I don't think so. His father will be angry if I buy him one of those. Have you got anything educational? You see, he's a very intelligent boy.

Assistant I've got the perfect thing! A do-it-yourself computer kit!

nephew
niece
grandson
grand-daughter

64 Made in England

Ken I like your radio. Is it new?
Pat Yes, I bought it last week. It's a Bisonic.
Ken Bisonic? I've never heard of it. Where was it made?
Pat I'm not sure. I think it was made in Japan. I'll have a look. No, I'm wrong. It was made in England.

Where was your	watch	made?
	pen	
	pencil	
	shirt	
	dress	
	jacket	
	tie	

Where were your	shoes	made?
	socks	
	jeans	
	glasses	
	trousers	

| (I think) | it was | made in (England). |
| | they were | |

| I don't know | where | it was | made. |
| I'm not sure | | they were | |

Questions

In your house, is there a television/cooker/refrigerator/washing machine/clock/camera/cassette-player/vacuum cleaner/hair-dryer/electric fire?

Where was it made?

Questions

Rolls-Royce cars are made in England.

What about Toyotas/Fiats/Volkswagens/Renaults/Chevrolets/Volvos?

What about Omega watches/Sony televisions/Parker pens/Boeing planes/Kodak cameras/IBM typewriters/Honda motor-cycles/Philips cassettes/Ronson lighters?

Questions

A lot of things are made in England – cars, planes, televisions, boats.

What things are made in your country/town/capital city?

Questions

England imports a lot of goods.
Coffee is imported from Brazil.

Make sentences using:
tea/India   beef/Argentina
wood/Sweden   oil/Saudi Arabia
wine/Spain   rubber/Malaysia

In your country what goods are imported?
Where are they imported from?
What things are exported from your country?

Questions

Milk	is	produced on English farms.
Butter		
Cheese		
Wheat		
Lamb		

Eggs	are	produced on English farms.
Potatoes		
Cabbages		
Cucumbers		
Lettuces		
Carrots		

| What | is | produced on farms in your country? |
| | are | |

Exercise

Clothes are washed at *the launderette*.

Films are shown at . . . .   hairdresser's
Newspapers are sold at . . . .   bank
Cars are repaired at . . . .   cinema
Hair is cut at . . . .   launderette
Photographs are taken at . . . .   studio
Bread is sold at . . . .   garage
Money is changed at . . . .   baker's
                                    newsagent's

Quiz

1	The first book was printed in	France	☐	Germany	☐	England	☐
2	Jaguar cars are made in	England	☐	The U.S.A.	☐	Italy	☐
3	John F. Kennedy was assassinated in	Houston	☐	New York	☐	Dallas	☐
4	Mount Everest was climbed for the first time in	1953	☐	1961	☐	1957	☐
5	The Eiffel Tower was built in	1876	☐	1889	☐	1901	☐
6	The motor car was invented in	1850	☐	1885	☐	1903	☐
7	Christopher Columbus was born in	Spain	☐	Italy	☐	Portugal	☐
8	Uranium was discovered in	1932	☐	1798	☐	1944	☐
9	Coffee is produced in	Colombia	☐	Scotland	☐	Canada	☐
10	Australia was discovered in	the 17th century	☐	the 16th century	☐	the 18th century	☐

Answers: 1 Germany 2 England 3 Dallas 4 1953 5 1889 6 1885 7 Italy 8 1798 9 Colombia 10 The 17th century

65 A real bargain

Mr Palmer is looking for a new house. He's tired of living in the city and he wants to live in a quiet village. He's with the estate agent now.

Estate Agent Well, Mr Palmer. This is the semi-detached house that I told you about . . . Number 26, Richmond Road. The owners are away, but I've got a key.

Mr Palmer Hmm . . . when was it built?

Agent It was built in 1928.

Mr Palmer Who built it?

Agent I'm not really sure. Is it important?

Mr Palmer No, not really. Is that a new roof? It looks new.

Agent It is nearly new. It was put on last year.

Agent You can see that it's in very good condition. The previous owner was a builder.

Mr Palmer It's quite an old house. I'm worried about the electrical wiring. Has it been rewired?

Agent Yes, it has.

Mr Palmer Oh, when was it done?

Agent Five years ago. Also, it's been redecorated. Central heating has been put in, and a new garage has been built.

Mr Palmer Oh, when was that done?

Agent Last year . . . I think.

Agent It's a very solid house. It's built of brick with a tiled roof . . .

Mr Palmer It's a long way from a big town. What are the services like?

Agent Hold on . . . I've got the details here. Yes . . . let me see . . . the dustbins are emptied every Thursday.

Mr Palmer It's important for me to see the post before I go to work. When is it delivered?

Agent It's usually delivered at about 7.30. The milk is delivered about six o'clock . . . so you'll have fresh milk for breakfast.

Mr Palmer It's certainly very cheap. I've seen a lot of similar houses . . . and they're more expensive.

Agent Ah, yes . . . it's a real bargain.

Mr Palmer Are there any plans for the area?

Agent Pardon? Plans . . . well, a new school is going to be built in the village next year . . .

Mr Palmer Anything else?

Agent . . . and a new road, a motorway actually, will be built next year, too. You'll be able to get to London easily.

Mr Palmer Where exactly will the motorway be built?

Agent Well, actually, it'll be built behind the house. A bridge will be constructed over the house. It'll be very interesting. You'll be able to watch the traffic . . . .

Exercise

13 Orchard Lane.
Cottage.
Built: 1820
Stone/thatched roof.
Central heating: 1978.
Rewired: 1972.

13 Orchard Lane is a cottage. It was built in 1820. It's built of stone with a thatched roof. Central heating was put in in 1978, and it was rewired in 1972.

Now write paragraphs about:

44 Primrose Avenue.
Detached house.
Built: 1935
Brick/tiled roof.
New roof: 1976
Redecorated: 1978

68 Jubilee Street.
Town house.
Built: 1977
Brick/flat roof.
Sauna: January 1978.
Repainted: May 1978.

66 The Eight O'Clock News

Good evening, and here is the Eight O'Clock News. Robert Gibbs, the great plane robber, has been caught in Montina. He was arrested in a Vanadelo night club. He is being questioned at police headquarters, and he will probably be sent back to Britain. Two British detectives left Heathrow earlier this evening, and they will help the police in Vanadelo with their enquiries. In 1978 Gibbs was sentenced to forty years in prison for his part in the Great Plane Robbery. He escaped from Parkwood Maximum Security Prison in April. Since then he has been seen in ten different countries.

The strike at Fernside Engineering in Birmingham has ended after talks between trade union leaders and management representatives. The strike began last weekend after a worker had been sacked. He had had an argument with a supervisor. Five thousand men went on strike. The worker has now been re-employed.

Vic Bostik, the lead guitarist of The Rats pop group, is dead. He was found unconscious in his Mayfair flat early this morning. Bostik was rushed to St. Swithin's Hospital, but doctors were unable to save his life. A number of bottles, which had been found in his flat, were taken away by the police.

There is no more news about the famous Lanstable painting, *Norfolk Sunset*, which was stolen last night from the National Gallery. The painting, which is worth half a million pounds, was given to the gallery in 1975. It hasn't been found yet, and all airports and ports are being watched. Cars and trucks are being searched. A reward of £10,000 has been offered for information.

Jumbo, the Indian elephant which escaped from London zoo this afternoon, has been caught. Jumbo was chased across Regent's Park, and was finally captured at a hot dog stall in Regent's Park Road. A tranquillizer gun was used, and Jumbo was loaded onto a truck and was taken back to the zoo. At the zoo, he was examined by the zoo veterinary surgeon. Fortunately no damage had been done, and Jumbo will be returned to the elephant house later tonight.

Jimmy MacTavish, the Eastfield United and Scotland striker, has been transferred. The contract was signed at lunchtime. He was transferred to the American club, Miami Galaxy, for $3,000,000. MacTavish, aged 23, was bought two years ago for a fee of £2000 from a Scottish non-league club.

Look at this

| Someone did it. | We don't know who did it.
or
It isn't important who did it.
or
We aren't interested in who did it. | It was done. |

(or *We are more interested in what was done than in who did it.*)

Someone does it . . . . .It is done.
Someone is doing it . . . . .It is being done.
Someone has done it . . . . . . .It has been done.
Someone had done it . . . . . . .It had been done.
Someone will do it . . . . .It will be done.

Exercise 1

Someone stole them. *They were stolen.*

Someone has found it.
Someone is watching it.
Someone cleans the windows.
Someone had taken them.
Someone will buy it.
Someone brought it.
Someone has seen it.
Someone is searching them.
Someone had caught it.
Someone will send it.

Exercise 2

Now write the news for today.

REVIEWS

FILMS

Monsters of the Deep
Produced by Anton Wells.
Directed by Stephen Slovanski.
Written by Harvey Foster.
Music composed by Oliver
Lawrence.

Monsters of the Deep, which is now
being shown at the Odeon,
Leicester Square, is one of the most
exciting films I've ever seen. It was
made in Hollywood last year, but the
sharks were filmed on location off
the coast of Florida. Steve Newman
is brilliant as the shark hunter, but
the real stars are the sharks themselves. It can be seen at cinemas in
the provinces from next week.
Don't miss it!

BOOKS

Atlantic Crossing
Written by Eric Redwood.
Published by Heath Brothers
(£12.95)

This book tells the story of Eric
Redwood who crossed the Atlantic
Ocean alone in a small wooden boat.
The boat was made in Ireland, and
was designed like the boats which
were used by Irish fisherman one
thousand years ago. Redwood
thinks America was first discovered
many years before Columbus was
born. The designs for the boat were
taken from old books which had
been found in an Irish monastery.
The book is beautifully illustrated
with many colour photographs and
maps. The photographs were taken
by Redwood himself during the
voyage.

RECORDS

Songs of the City
By Lisa Francis (XYZ Records)
Produced by Martin Duncan.

All the songs on this new album
were written by Lisa herself, and the
album was recorded live during her
recent successful concert tour. She is
accompanied by several well-
known musicians, Elton Kash,
Dave Langdown, Ken Thompson,
and Tony Lloyd. There is a great
variety of music on the album—
gentle romantic ballads, soul music,
and exciting rock songs. The words
to all the songs are printed on the
back of the cover.

TELEVISION

Last of the Eagles?
Directed by Barbara Anfield.
(BBC-TV)

This documentary, which was first
shown on BBC 2 last year, will be
repeated on BBC 1 next week. The
golden eagle is now found in only a
few remote places in Scotland. In
recent years nests have been robbed
and eggs have been stolen. Eagles
are protected by law, but they are
threatened with extinction. Barbara
Anfield spent a year making this
programme. The everyday habits of
the eagle have been recorded for
future generations.

Exercise

Now write a short review of
 a film that you've seen.
 a book that you've read.
 a record that you've heard.
 a television programme that you've seen.

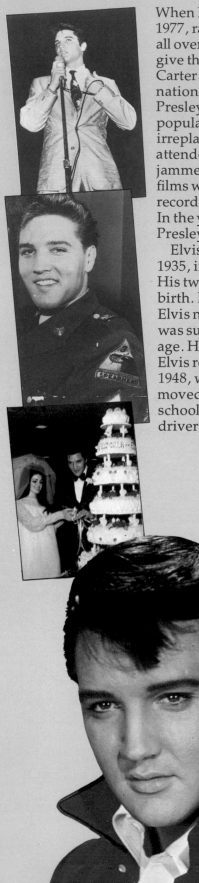

When Elvis Presley died on 16th August, 1977, radio and television programmes all over the world were interrupted to give the news of his death. President Carter was asked to declare a day of national mourning. Carter said: 'Elvis Presley changed the face of American popular culture. . . . He was unique and irreplaceable.' Eighty thousand people attended his funeral. The streets were jammed with cars, and Elvis Presley films were shown on television, and his records were played on the radio all day. In the year after his death, 100 million Presley LPs were sold.

Elvis Presley was born on January 8th, 1935, in Tupelo, Mississippi. His twin brother, Jesse Garon, died at birth. His parents were very poor and Elvis never had music lessons, but he was surrounded by music from an early age. His parents were very religious, and Elvis regularly sang at church services. In 1948, when he was thirteen, his family moved to Memphis, Tennessee. He left school in 1953 and got a job as a truck driver.

In the summer of 1953 Elvis paid $4 and recorded two songs for his mother's birthday at Sam Phillips' Sun Records studio. Sam Phillips heard Elvis and asked him to record *That's All Right* in July 1954. 20,000 copies were sold, mainly in and around Memphis. He made five more records for Sun, and in July 1955 he met Colonel Tom Parker, who became his manager in November. Parker sold Elvis's contract to RCA Records. Sun Records got $35,000 and Elvis got $5,000. With the money he bought a pink Cadillac for his mother. On January 10th, 1956, Elvis recorded *Heartbreak Hotel*, and a million copies were sold. In the next fourteen months he made another fourteen records, and they were all big hits. In 1956 he also made his first film in Hollywood.

In March, 1958, Elvis had to join the army. He wanted to be an ordinary soldier. When his hair was cut thousands of women cried. He spent the next two years in Germany, where he met Priscilla Beaulieu, who became his wife eight years later on May 1st, 1967. In 1960 he left the army and went to Hollywood where he made several films during the next few years.

By 1968 many people had become tired of Elvis. He hadn't performed live since 1960. But he recorded a new LP *From Elvis in Memphis* and appeared in a special television programme. He became popular again, and went to Las Vegas, where he was paid $750,000 for four weeks. In 1972 his wife left him, and they were divorced in October, 1973. He died from a heart attack. He had been working too hard, and eating and drinking too much for several years. He left all his money to his only daughter, Lisa Marie Presley. She became one of the richest people in the world when she was only nine years old.

69 If I had enough money . . .

Andrew

I've got £3500. I'm going to look at the car. If I like it, I'll buy it.

How much is the car?
Has he got enough money?
Is he going to look at the car?
Will he buy it?
What will he do if he likes it?

> **FORD CORTINA.** For Sale. One careful lady owner. Very good condition. £3,500

Barbara

That's a nice car, but I haven't got enough money.
If I had enough money, I'd buy it!

Does she like the car?
Has she got enough money?
Will she buy the car? Why not?
What would she do if she had enough money?

Christopher

I've worked for an oil company for ten years.
I'm a Bachelor of Science in Engineering.
I've got the qualifications.
I'm going to apply for the job.
If they offer me the job, I'll certainly take it.

Has he got experience?
Has he got a B.Sc?
Is he going to apply?
What will he do, if they offer him the job?

> **ENGINEER WANTED** North Sea oil company. Qualifications: Bachelor of Science and five years experience of similar work.

David

I like that job, but I can't apply for it.
I haven't got the qualifications.
If I had the qualifications, I'd apply for it.

Does he like the job?
Can he apply?
Why not?
What would he do, if he had the qualifications?

Eric

I'm a mechanic, and I know a lot about cars.
I've got a clean driving licence and enough money.
If they ask me, I'll go with them.

What's his job?
How much does he know about cars?
Has he got a clean driving licence?
Has he got enough money?
What'll he do, if they ask him to go with them?

> **OVERLAND EXPEDITION** TO AUSTRALIA. By Land Rover. Three men wanted. QUALIFICATIONS—clean driving licence – mechanical knowledge. The applicant must have £1,000 for expenses.

Frank

I've got £1000, and a driving licence.
But I know very little about cars.
If I knew something about cars, I'd go with them.

Has he got a licence?
What about money?
How much does he know about cars?
What would he do if he knew enough about cars?

Georgina

I can speak French and German.
I'll apply for the job.
If I get it, I'll have to move to Switzerland.

What languages can she speak?
What languages does she need?
Will she apply?
What'll she do if she gets the job?

> **WANTED** Secretary for busy office in Geneva. The applicant must be able to speak French and German. Apply: UNO, WHO, Geneva.

Helen

I can speak French, but I can't speak German.
If I could speak German, I would apply for the job.

Can she speak German?
Does she need German?
Can she apply?
Why not?
What would she do, if she could speak German?

Isabel

I'm 19 and I'm interested in the job.
I'll get more information if I phone them, and if the salary's good I'll apply!

How old is she?
Is she too old?
What'll happen if she phones?
Will she apply?

> **TRAINEE COMPUTER PROGRAMMER.** A marvellous opportunity for a young person aged between 18 & 23. For more information: Phone 01-123 4567

Jack

I'm interested in the job, but I'm too old.
If I were younger, I'd apply.

Is he over 23 or under 23?
Is he going to apply?
Why not?
What would he do, if he were younger?

If	I	had enough money,	I	'd	buy that car.
	you	were rich,	you	would	travel.
	we		we		etc.
	they		they		
	he		he		
	she		she		

70 In a restaurant

Waiter Good evening, sir . . . madam.
Shall I take your coats?
Mr Adams Thank you. Where shall we
sit, Barbara?
Waiter Oh, would you like to sit over
here, sir? Near the window.
Mr Adams Ah, yes. . . . Could we see the
menu?
Waiter Certainly. Here it is.

near the window
near the door
at the side
in the middle

Mr Adams Do you fancy a starter?
Mrs Adams Mmm . . . I think I'll have the
prawn cocktail. I'm very fond of
prawns. What about you?
Mr Adams I'm not sure . . . I can't decide.
Mrs Adams Oh, I'd have the trout, if I
were you. You always say that you like
trout, and you haven't had it for a long
time.

Waiter Are you ready to order yet, sir?
Mr Adams Yes . . . a prawn cocktail for
my wife, and the trout for me.
Waiter And the main course, sir?
Mr Adams Veal for my wife. I can't
decide between the veal and the
chicken. What do you recommend?
Waiter Oh, if I were you, I'd have the
veal. It's the speciality of the house.

Waiter What would you like with the
veal?
Mr Adams Two mixed salads, please.
Waiter . . . any vegetables, sir?
Mr Adams Yes. Some cauliflower, some
courgettes and some boiled potatoes,
please.
Waiter Anything to follow?
Mr Adams Can we order that later?
Waiter Of course, sir.

Waiter Would you like to see the wine
list?
Mr Adams Yes . . . we'd like a bottle of
dry white wine.
Waiter May I suggest something?
Mr Adams Of course.
Waiter Why don't you try a bottle of
English wine?
Mr Adams English wine?
Waiter Yes, it isn't very well-known, but
it's being produced in the south of
England now. You'll be surprised . . .
it's very good.

MENU

STARTERS

Prawn Cocktail £1·50
French Onion Soup £0·75
Pâté £1·00
Melon £0·85
Trout £2·00
Fruit Juice 50p
Avocado with Prawns £1·00

MAIN COURSES

Veal (in cream sauce with brandy) £3·10
Chicken (fried in breadcrumbs) £2·50
Steak (in red wine sauce with mushrooms)
£3·50
Scampi (served with tomato and garlic sauce, and rice) £3·45
Roast Beef (with Yorkshire pudding)
£3·60

SALADS — mixed, green, tomato £0·75
VEGETABLES —
Cauliflower £0·50   Brussels Sprouts £0·50
Courgettes   £0·60   Peas   £0·40
Greenbeans   £0·50   Carrots £0·40
Potatoes — boiled, French fried, roast, baked £0·50

WINES

Muscadet (French)   Mosel (German)
Beaulieu (English)   Graves (French)
Soave (Italian)

71 North Sea Oil

Good evening. This is London Radio. Welcome to 'Man in the Street'. Our programme tonight is about North Sea oil. Oil was first discovered beneath the North Sea in the late 1960s. Since then more and more oil has been found off the coasts of Britain, and is being brought ashore. We aren't going to become very rich, but we must decide how to spend the oil revenues. Our interviewer went into the streets to ask people their opinion. He asked: 'If you were the Prime Minister, what would you do with the money?'

'Well, of course I'm not the Prime Minister, but if I were, I'd spend the money on more hospitals and schools. We need more doctors, nurses, and teachers. Classes are too big. If classes were smaller, children would learn more. And there aren't enough nurses either, because salaries are too low. If the salaries were higher, more people would become nurses. Money which is spent now on education and health is an investment for the future.'

'I think the answer is quite simple. Taxes are much too high in this country, aren't they? I would reduce them. If we reduced taxes, people would have more money. If they had more money, they'd spend more. Industry would have to produce more, so it would need more workers. There would be more jobs, and we would all be richer.'

'I'm very worried about inflation. I'd try to control prices. If I were the Prime Minister, I'd reduce the price of gas, coal, and electricity. If we did that, everybody would benefit, wouldn't they? Food is much too expensive. I'd encourage the farmers to produce more food, more cheaply. However there are some things that I certainly wouldn't do. I certainly wouldn't build more roads, and I wouldn't spend money on guns, and tanks, and warplanes.'

'There's too much crime and violence nowadays. There aren't enough policemen on the streets. I'd increase the size of the police force, and I'd increase their salaries. If we had more policemen, we'd all feel safer. I'd also increase old age pensions. I've worked hard all my life, and I should have a reasonable standard of living.'

Exercise

If you were the Prime Minister or President of your country, what would you do?

72 What would you do?

Imagine that you are going to a desert island. You can take six things. Which six things would you take? And why?

If I weren't here, I'd like to be in California.

If you weren't here, where would you like to be? Why?

If I could be somebody else, I'd like to be a filmstar.

If you could be somebody else, who would you like to be? Why?

If I had a million pounds, I'd travel round the world.

If you had a million pounds, what would you do? Why?

If I were you...

I've got a headache. *If I were you, I'd* | *take an aspirin.*
see a doctor.
have a rest.
go for a walk, etc.

I want to buy a pet. If you were me, which pet would you buy? Why?
I also want to buy a radio/a car/a watch/a camera/an English book.
Give me some advice.

Now advise these people:

I've lost my passport.

I've been bitten by a snake.

I can't sleep at night.

I want to win an Olympic medal.

I've cut myself.

I've just seen an accident.

I need some money and the banks are shut.

I want to stop smoking.

I want to be a millionaire.

I've been mugged!

I don't know what to wear...

I'm going to have tea with the Queen, and I don't know what to wear!
I'm going to a wedding/a funeral/a discotheque/a football match/Honolulu/the North Pole/England/the Moon.
Give me some advice.

I don't know what to buy...

It's my mother's birthday tomorrow, and I don't know what to buy!
It's my father's birthday next week. He'll be 47.
It's my brother's birthday next month. He'll be 16.
It's my sister's birthday on Thursday. She'll be 21.
It's my baby brother's birthday tomorrow. He'll be 3.
It's my little sister's birthday on Sunday. She'll be 10.
Give me some advice.

What would you do? What wouldn't you do?

Look at this

It's important to do it. Someone must do it . . . it must be done.
It's impossible. Nobody can do it . . . it can't be done.
It was impossible. Nobody could do it . . . it couldn't be done.
It's possible. Someone may do it . . . it may be done.

74 Four reports

Laura Bruce is a trainee reporter for the *London Evening Echo*. Last week several famous people arrived at London Airport. Laura was sent to interview them. Nobody told her very much!

Doctor Sowanso, Secretary-General, UNO:
'I'm very busy. I've got a lot of appointments. I can't say very much. I love England. I've been here many times before. I enjoyed my visit in January. I'll only be in England for twelve hours. I'm going to meet the Prime Minister. I have no other comments.'

Laura's Report
Dr Sowanso visited England yesterday. He arrived at London Airport at 10 am, and we asked him to comment on the international situation. He just made a brief statement. He said he was very busy, and that he'd got a lot of appointments. He said he couldn't say very much, but he said he loved England. He said that he had been here many times, and that he had enjoyed his visit in January. He said he would be in England for only twelve hours, and that he was going to meet the Prime Minister. He said he had no other comments.

Brutus Cray, world champion boxer:
'I like newspaper reporters, but I haven't got time to say much. Just that I'm the greatest! I've always been the greatest, and I always will be the greatest. I can beat anybody in the world! I've beaten Leo Fink before. I knocked him out in Miami, and I'm going to knock him out in São Paulo. I'll be the champion forever! Excuse me. . . .'

Laura's Report
Brutus Cray stopped at London Airport on his way from Frankfurt to São Paulo. I managed to see him in the V.I.P. lounge. Brutus was in a hurry. He said he liked newspaper reporters, but that he hadn't got time to say much. He said he was the greatest, he had always been the greatest, and he always would be the greatest. He said he could beat anybody in the world. He also said he had beaten Leo Fink before. He said he had knocked Fink out in Miami, and that he was going to knock him out in São Paulo. He also said he would be the champion forever!

Look at this

Maria said, "It's my car."	She said it was her car.
John said, "I like England."	He said he liked England.
Anne said, "I can swim."	She said she could swim.
Paul said, "I've got a new car."	He said he had got a new car.
Wendy said, "I've been to Paris."	She said she had been to Paris.
Mike said, "I bought it in London."	He said he had bought it in London.
Jean said, "I'll go to New York."	She said she would go to New York.

Exercise
Now, write reports on these statements, which were also made to Laura at London Airport:

Elton Kash, pop star
'I'm not staying in England long.
I'm on my way to the United States.
I'm going to record another album.
I've written ten new songs.
I like recording in Detroit.
I made my last album there.
I'll be in Detroit for six weeks.'

Stanley Walsh, ex-footballer
'I don't like reporters.
They've written a lot of lies about me.
They destroyed my marriage.
I've got a new career.
I'm tired of football.
I'll never play in England again.
I can't say anything more.'

75 Examination day

Victor Hey, Maria! Have you finished your exam?

Maria Yes, I have.

Victor Was it difficult?

Maria Well, it was quite hard.

Victor Did you pass?

Maria I don't know . . . she didn't tell me.

Victor What questions did she ask?

Maria First she asked me what my name was.

Victor That was easy, wasn't it?

Maria . . . then she asked me where I came from, and how long I'd been studying at the school.

Victor . . . and what else did she ask?

Maria She asked when I had begun studying English, and she asked how I would use English in the future.

Victor Go on . . .

Maria Then she asked me if I liked the school, and if I lived with my parents.

Victor Anything else?

Maria Oh, Victor! I'm trying to remember . . . oh, yes! She asked if I spoke any other languages.

Victor Is that all?

Maria Oh, there were a lot of other questions. She asked me what my hobbies were, and she asked me to tell her about them. Then she gave me a picture and asked me to describe it. Oh, and then I was asked to read a passage.

Victor What did she say at the end?

Maria Ah! She asked me to tell you to go in . . . immediately.

This is the paper that the examiner used, when she was asking the questions.

UNIVERSITY OF WESSEX

Examination in English as a Foreign Language

Stage One: Oral Examination.

This list must not be shown to the candidates

☑ 1 What's your name?
☑ 2 Where do you come from?
☑ 3 How long have you been studying at the school?
☑ 4 When did you begin?
☐ 5 How will you use English in the future?
☐ 6 Do you like the school?
☐ 7 Do you live with your parents?
☐ 8 Do you speak any other languages?
☐ 9 What are your hobbies? Tell me about them.
☐ 10 Look at this picture. Describe it.
☐ 11 Reading passage

Look at this

"Do you like English food?" . . . . (She) asked (him) if (he) liked English food.

"Have you been to Paris?" . . . . (He) asked (me) if (I had) been to Paris.

"Will you go there?" . . . . (They) asked (us) if (we) would go there.

"What's your address?" . . . . (I) asked (them) what (their) address was.

"How did you come to school?" . . . . (You) asked (her) how (she) had come to school.

"When can you do it?" . . . . (She) asked (me) when (I) could do it.

76 But you said . . .

Marion Good afternoon.
Travel Agent Good afternoon, madam.
Marion I'm interested in the holiday in Saint Cuthbert.
Agent Ah, yes . . . the Caribbean! I can recommend it highly.
Marion Can you tell me a little bit more about it?
Agent Of course, madam. It's an excellent package holiday.
You'll travel on a scheduled flight. You'll be met at the
airport, and taken to your hotel. You won't have to pay
airport taxes. They're included in the price. The hotel is very
near the beach, and it's got a swimming pool and a
discotheque. It's a very modern hotel, it was built last year.
The restaurant's superb, and drinks are very cheap in Saint
Cuthbert. Oh, and you can walk to the sea in two minutes.
Marion Hmm . . . it sounds good. I'd like to make a
reservation.
Agent One moment, madam and I'll get you a booking form.

Marion paid a deposit, and booked the holiday. Two months
later she was in Saint Cuthbert. But she was disappointed.
When she returned to England, she went to see the travel
agent.

Agent Ah! It's Miss Ward. Did you have a good holiday?
Marion No, I certainly did not have a good holiday.
Agent Oh, I'm very sorry to hear that. What was wrong?
Marion Well, when I arrived in Saint Cuthbert, I had to spend
four hours at the airport . . . you said that we would be met,
and we weren't. You also said that we would be taken to the
hotel. We weren't and the taxi cost about £12. You told me
that airport taxes were included. In fact I had to pay £10.
Agent Oh, dear . . . you had a very bad start. But the hotel was
nice, wasn't it?
Marion No, it was not! You said it was very modern. You were
quite right. They hadn't finished building it! We couldn't
sleep because the workmen were working all night . . . on
our balcony! You said it had got a swimming pool. It had . . .
but it was empty. And the restaurant . . . the restaurant
served fish every night.
Agent Oh, dear . . .
Marion You said that the hotel was near the beach, and that
we could walk to the sea in two minutes.
Agent Couldn't you?
Marion Well, yes . . . we could . . . but there was an oil refinery
between the hotel and the beach, and it took half an hour to
walk round it.
Agent Oh, I'm really terribly sorry. We really didn't know . . . .
I'm afraid we're unable to give you a refund, but we can give
you a ten per cent discount on next year's holiday . . . .
Marion Next year! Next year, I'm staying in England!

Exercise

This is an advertisement for another holiday.
Jane went there. None of the things the agent
said were true.
*You said the hotel had got three bars and a
restaurant, but it hadn't.*
You said we would love the food, but we didn't.

Write down her other complaints to the travel
agent.

Come to Sunny **MANDANGA**

Ten good reasons for a visit
to the Hotel Superb:

1 You'll enjoy the scenery.
2 The weather is excellent.
3 You'll love the food.
4 You can go riding.
5 You'll be met at the airport.
6 All the hotel staff are friendly.
7 The hotel has got three bars and a restaurant.
8 Every room has got a shower.
9 You can see the beach from the hotel.
10 There are excursions every day.

77 Having things done

A Sorry I'm late. I couldn't start the car this morning.

B Well, winter's coming. It was probably cold.

A It needs a service, really . . . but garages are so expensive nowadays.

B Can't you service it yourself?

A Who? Me? I don't know anything about cars!

B Then if I were you, I'd have it serviced. The garage that I use is very reasonable. And have the radiator filled with anti-freeze. They say it's going to be a cold winter.

radiator/filled with anti-freeze
brakes/tested
battery/checked
oil/changed
tyres/checked

C Do you know where there's a good dry-cleaner's?

D Yes . . . there's a good one in Victoria Road. I'd go there if I were you.

C Oh, thanks. I want to have my suit cleaned . . . I'm going to a wedding on Saturday.

D Well, I had my suit cleaned there last week, and they did a good job.

suit
jacket
skirt
dress
trousers

a wedding
a funeral
a party
a dance

E Excuse me. Do you do alterations?

F Yes, we do. What kind of alteration do you want?

E I'd like to have this skirt lengthened. It's too short for me.

F That's fine. It'll take about a fortnight.

E . . . and at the same time I want to have this dress shortened. It's a bit too long.

F Good. Would you mind just putting the skirt on first? There's a changing room over there.

a fortnight
three days
a week
ten days

skirt/dress
trousers/jeans
jacket/coat
overcoat/raincoat

G Hello. Can I make an appointment to see the optician?

H Yes. Would next Friday be convenient? At three o'clock?

G Oh, yes. I want to have my eyes tested. I think I need some new glasses. Goodbye.

H Goodbye. Oh, be careful! That isn't the door! It's a window!

G Oh, yes. . . . Sorry!

optician
eyes tested
doctor
blood pressure tested
dentist
tooth filled
dentist
some dentures made

79 The Appointment

Once upon a time, there was a rich Caliph in Baghdad. He was very famous because he was wise and kind. One morning he sent his servant, Abdul, to the market to buy some fruit. As Abdul was walking through the market, he suddenly felt very cold. He knew that somebody was behind him. He turned round and saw a tall man, dressed in black. He couldn't see the man's face, only his eyes. The man was staring at him, and Abdul began to shiver.
'Who are you? What do you want?' Abdul asked.
The man in black didn't reply.
'What's your name?' Abdul asked nervously.
'I . . . am . . . Death,' the stranger replied coldly and turned away.

Abdul dropped his basket and ran all the way back to the Caliph's house. He rushed into the Caliph's room.
'Excuse me, master. I have to leave Baghdad immediately,' Abdul said.
'But why? What's happened?' the Caliph asked.
'I've just met Death in the market,' Abdul replied.
'Are you certain?' said the Caliph.
'Yes, I'm certain. He was dressed in black, and he stared at me. I'm going to my father's house in Samarra. If I go at once, I'll be there before sunset.'
The Caliph could see that Abdul was terrified and gave him permission to go to Samarra.

The Caliph was puzzled. He was fond of Abdul and he was angry because Abdul had been badly frightened by the stranger in the market. He decided to go to the market and investigate. When he found the man in black, he spoke to him angrily.
'Why did you frighten my servant?'
'Who is your servant?' the stranger replied.
'His name is Abdul,' answered the Caliph.
'I didn't want to frighten him. I was just surprised to see him in Baghdad.'
'Why were you surprised?' the Caliph asked.
'I was surprised because I've got an appointment with him . . . tonight . . . in Samarra!'

Exercise

'Excuse me, master. I have to leave Baghdad immediately,' Abdul said.
Abdul said that he had to leave Baghdad immediately.

Now, change the three conversations into reported speech.

80 The last letter from Paris

68 rue des Alpes,
Paris.
October 18th.

Dear John,

It was so nice to see you last week. After you had gone I felt so lonely. I still do. I really enjoyed seeing you again. I hope you enjoyed yourself, too.

Two days ago I took my final exam, and it was pretty difficult. The papers are being marked now. My teacher told me that I would probably pass. I hope so! If I pass, I'll get a certificate. It'll be very useful... I'll be able to get a better job.

When you phoned you said that you'd got a new job. You didn't tell me much about it. Do you like it? You said that you were working very hard. If I were you, I wouldn't work too hard!

Last night we had a farewell class party. We went to a new riverside restaurant that was opened last month. The atmosphere was great! Everyone was in a good mood because they'd finished the course. I'm going to miss all the new friends that I've made here. I must stop writing now, John. I'm going to have my hair done this afternoon. I hope it won't be too expensive! See you next week. I hope you'll be able to meet me at the airport.

All my love,
Mary

P.S. I've had my portrait painted by a street artist in Montmartre.

Exercise

Now write John's reply to Mary:
Write your address and the date/Begin *Dear Mary*/Tell her that you were pleased to receive her letter/Tell her that you miss her/Ask her if she's passed her exam/Tell her that you think she'll be able to get a better job/Tell her about your new job/Ask her what time she'll arrive at the airport/Tell her that you'll be able to meet her/Say that you've just bought a car/Tell her that it's a very old car/Explain that you're going to have it repainted/Send her all your love/Sign your name/Write a postscript and tell her that you've had your photograph taken.

Vocabulary

This vocabulary contains all the words in the student's book, and the number of the unit where they first occur.

A

a 1
A272 50
(be) able to 15
aboard 1
about 1
absolutely 41
accent 45
accept 46
accident 4
accompany 67
accounts 2
across 66
actress 30
'ad' 15
address 1
(in) advance 46
adventure 47
advertisement 53
advice 38
advise (v) 63
afraid 21
African 7
after 7
afternoon 9
again 6
against 21
age 19
aged 66
ago 10
agree 33
air 12, 37
airport 5
alarm clock 61
album (record) 63
alcohol 38
alibi 28
all 1
all right 2
almost 56
alone 5
Alsatian (dog) 27
alteration 77
always 6
am 1
American 1
ambulance 60
amuse 37
an 1
and 1
angry 21
animal 12
anniversary 26
announcer 23
announcement 25
another 1
answer (n) 6
answer (v) 13
anti-freeze 77
any 3
any more 34
anything 10
anyway 21
apartment 30
application form 22
apply 22
appointment 46
approach (v) 57
approximately 25
Arabic 53
are 1
area 2
argument 30
arm (n) 12
armchair 40

army 15
Army Careers
  Office 15
around 1
arrange 51
arrest 41
arrive 6
article 40
artificial 60
artist 80
as 6
Ascot races 28
ashore 71
ashtray 63
Asian 7
ask 1
asleep 42
aspirin 72
assassinate 64
astonished 54
astronaut 12
at 2
atmosphere 80
attack 37
attempt 4
attend 68
Australia House 16
Australian 1
automatic 3
autumn 47
available 53
Ave. (avenue) 50
average 4
avocado 70
away 4
awful 1

B

B.A. 61
  (Bachelor of Arts)
baby 6
back 8
backache 9
bad 6
badly 8
bag 9
baked 70
baker 64
balcony 76
bald 54
ballad 67
ballet 46
band 55
bandage 26
bank 1
bar 4, 76
bargain 65
bar of soap 9
basement 50
basket 60
bass 11
bath (v) 6
bathroom 29
battery 58
be 1
beach 19
bean 70
beard 42
beat (v) 74
beautiful 48
beautifully 67
because 12
become 68

bed 1
bedroom 29
bedside 55
beef 64
been 1
beer 28
before 4
begin 23
beginning 37
behind 28
believe 13
bell 23
belong 53
below 54
bend (n) 57
beneath 71
benefit 71
beside 62
best 3
bet 57
better 3
between 20
big 19
bill (n) 18
bird 13
birth 1
birthday 28
(a) bit 27
bite (v) 27
black 8
blame 73
bleed 26
block 73
blonde 41
blood 37
blood pressure 77
blue 9
board (v) 25
boarding card 1
boat 42
boiled 70
bomb (n) 73
boo (v) 21
book (n) 41
book (v) 19
booking form 79
border 36
bore (v) 37
boring 6
born 1
borrow 43
boss 14
both 3
bother (v) 50
bottles 26
bottom 20
box 9
boxer 74
boy 27
boyfriend 35
bracelet 63
brakes 77
brand new 11
brandy 29
bread 38
breadcrumbs 70
break 39
breakdown 42, 58
breakfast 42
breast stroke 4
breathe 12
brick 65
bridge 44
brief 74
bright 48
brilliant 67
bring 13
bristle 9
Britain 4
brochure 19

brown 61
Brussels sprouts 70
B.Sc. 69
  (Bachelor of Science)
budgie 27
buffet 13
build (v) 64
building 23
burn (v) 60
bus 8
business 2
busy 7
but 4
butter 64
button 56
buy (v) 3
buzzer 55
by 4
by the way 1

C

°C (centigrade) 19
cabbage 64
cable (n) 18
cabin 1
cafeteria 50
caliph 79
call (n) 2
call (v) 13
calmly 23
camera 64
cameraman 21
can (v) 2
can (n) 58
Canadian 1
canal 19
cane 44
capital 64
capsule 9
captain 1
capture (v) 66
car 10
card 1
care (v) 30
career 74
careful 26
carefully 12
careless 20
carelessly 20
cargo 53
carrier-bag 54
carrot 64
carry (v) 13
case 13
cash (n) 18
cash (v) 18
cassette 64
cassette-player 45
casualty 55
cat 13
catch (v) 6
cauliflower 70
cause (v) 23
ceiling 13
centimetre 4
central 28
central heating 65
centre 16
certain 33
certainly 4
certificate 80
chain 63
chair 8
champagne 26
champion 74
change (v) 8
charge (n) 2
chart 63
chase (v) 66

cheap 49
cheaply 71
check (v) 18
check in 25
cheer (v) 21
cheese 64
chef 49
chemist 8
cheque 18
cheque book 58
chicken 28
child 62
children 3
chips 28
choose 27
Christmas 63
church 27
cigarette 27
cigarette case 25
cinema 31
city 16
class 61
clean 3
clean (v) 6
cleaner (n) 6
clear 27
clearly 51
clever 12
cliff 53
climb (v) 12
clock 2
close (v) 3
closed 48
close-up 21
cloth 49
clothes 3
cloud 12
cloudy 48
club 38
clue 73
cm. (centimetre) 19
coal 71
coast 25
coat 11
cocktail 6
coffee 3
coffee machine 3
code 2
cold (adj.) 11
cold (n) 9
coldly 79
collapse 23
collide 54
collision 53
colour 8
comb 25
come 1
come back 9
come in 17
come on! 6
comment (n) 73
company 2
comparison 20
compartment 3
competition 4
competitor 4
complain 34
complaint 73
complete (v) 1
complete (adj.) 61
compose 65
comprehensive 55
computer 12
concert 46
Concorde 27
condition 65
conduct 16
confirm 59
congratulations 26
connect 2

Irregular verbs

Infinitive form	Past tense	Past participle
be	was/were	been
beat	beat	beaten
become	became	become
begin	began	begun
bite	bit	bitten
break	broke	broken
bring	brought	brought
build	built	built
burn	burnt	burnt
buy	bought	bought
catch	caught	caught
choose	chose	chosen
come	came	come
cost	cost	cost
cut	cut	cut
do	did	done
drink	drank	drunk
drive	drove	driven
eat	ate	eaten
fall	fell	fallen
feel	felt	felt
fight	fought	fought
find	found	found
fly	flew	flown
forbid	forbade	forbidden
forget	forgot	forgotten
freeze	froze	frozen
get	got	got
give	gave	given
go	went	gone
grow	grew	grown
have	had	had
hear	heard	heard
hide	hid	hidden
hit	hit	hit
hurt	hurt	hurt
keep	kept	kept
know	knew	known
learn	learnt	learnt
leave	left	left
lend	lent	lent
let	let	let
light	lit	lit
lose	lost	lost
make	made	made
mean	meant	meant
meet	met	met
pay	paid	paid
put	put	put
read	read	read
ride	rode	ridden
ring	rang	rung
run	ran	run
say	said	said
see	saw	seen
sell	sold	sold
send	sent	sent
shine	shone	shone
shoot	shot	shot
show	showed	shown
shut	shut	shut
sing	sang	sung
sit	sat	sat
sleep	slept	slept
smell	smelt	smelt
speak	spoke	spoken
spend	spent	spent
stand	stood	stood
steal	stole	stolen
swim	swam	swum
take	took	taken
teach	taught	taught
tear	tore	torn
tell	told	told
think	thought	thought
throw	threw	thrown
wake	woke	woken
wear	wore	worn
win	won	won
write	wrote	written